The New Complete Book of Home Buying

The New Complete Book of Home Buying

Michael Sumichrast
Ronald G. Shafer
with
Martin A. Sumichrast

McGraw-Hill
New York   Chicago   San Francisco   Lisbon   London
Madrid   Mexico City   Milan   New Delhi
San Juan   Seoul   Singapore
Sydney   Toronto

1 2 3 4 5 6 7 8 9 0   DOC/DOC   0 9 8 7 6 5 4

ISBN 0-07-144487-4

This publication is designed to provide accurate and authoritative information in regard to the subject matter covered. It is sold with the understanding that the publisher is not engaged in rendering legal, accounting, or other professional service. If legal advice or other expert assistance is required, the services of a competent professional person should be sought.

> —*From a declaration of principles jointly adopted by a committee of the American Bar Association and a committee of publishers.*

McGraw-Hill books are available at special quantity discounts to use as premiums and sales promotions, or for use in corporate training programs. For more information, please write to the Director of Special Sales, Professional Publishing, McGraw-Hill, Two Penn Plaza, New York, NY 10121-2298. Or contact your local bookstore.

This book is printed on recycled, acid-free paper containing a minimum of 50% recycled, de-inked fiber.

Library of Congress Cataloging-in-Publication Data

Sumichrast, Michael.
   The new complete book of home buying/by Michael Sumichrast, Ronald G. Shafer and Martin A. Sumichrast.
     p. cm.
   ISBN 0-07-144487-4 (pbk. : alk. paper)
   1. House buying. 2. House selling. I. Shafer, Ronald G. II. Sumichrast, Martin A. III. Title.

   HD1379.S95 2004
   643'.12—dc22   2004007110

Contents

Preface   *vii*

Chapter 1   Home Sweet Home: Still the Best Investment   1
You Will Ever Make

Chapter 2   Holy Home Prices, or What Can You Afford?   19

Chapter 3   Home-Buying Strategies, or 50 Ways to Leave   47
Your Landlord or Your Old House

Chapter 4   Mouse Hunt, House Hunt: Shopping on the Internet   71

Chapter 5   Something Old or Something New: Existing   87
Houses versus New Houses

Chapter 6   Shopping for a Good Buy—from the Outside   111

Chapter 7   Shopping for a Good Buy—the Inside Story   133

Chapter 8   A Home Isn't Always a House—Condominiums   159
and Town Houses

Chapter 9   Negotiating the Best Deal   179

Chapter 10   How to Mortgage Your Future and   193
Find Happiness

Chapter 11   Protecting Yourself at Settlement: 215
The House Is Yours!

Index   *235*

Preface

The New Complete Book of Home Buying is an update of a classic for today's home-buying market. This book will guide you step by step through the home-buying process, whether you are a first-time buyer or are moving for the umpteenth time. What makes this book different is that it shows you how to treat your home purchase as an investment, because, in fact, a home is the biggest investment that most of us will ever make. And it is one of the few ways in which average Americans can accumulate assets.

That's why we were advocates of home buying back in the early 1980s, when best-selling books were warning people of economic doom and urging them to dump their houses and move into apartments. Our message at the time in *The Complete Book of Home Buying* was, in effect: The first thing you have to do is to make an irrevocable decision to buy a house. We don't care what kind of a house. It could be a small old or new house, a condo, a vacation home, or a town house. It could be a cheap house or a costlier home with a mortgage you can barely afford. It could be to live in or to rent out. Just buy a house. Do it as soon as possible. Do it while you are young—the younger, the better. Just do it. Believe us, it will more than pay off.

Did it ever. Between 1980 and 2004, the median home price more than tripled to over $170,000. We are still optimistic about home ownership. Chances are that you will never make a better investment. You can live in the house, work in the house, take advantage of tax breaks, and begin to pay off the mortgage instead of paying rent. Housing markets run hot and cold, but if you buy wisely, over time you are likely to see your house increasing in value.

This book will take you through the incredible increases in prices over the 25 years since we wrote our first book. These increases reflected everything from the consumer demand of the giant baby boom generation to increased housing regulations. During that time, *The Complete Book of Home Buying* became a classic. The original book was a Book-of-the-Month Club selection and a Fortune (magazine) Book Club selection. The original book and its updated version, published in the late 1980s, became the Bible of home buying for many in the baby boom generation. One Amazon.com buyer of the book called it "the BEST book for the home buyer" and added "buying a house without reading this book would be the biggest mistake you will ever make."

But the book you are reading is not your father's *Complete Book of Home Buying*. This book has been revamped and updated to meet the needs of today's home buyers. An entire chapter is devoted to the avalanche of information that is available on the Internet, a tool that didn't exist when we wrote our first book back in 1979. The book also examines new trends in housing—for instance, the rising values of condominiums and town houses, which in the past were the weak sisters in terms of housing-value appreciation. At the same time, this book lays out the unchanging fundamentals of home buying. We show you how to shop for the right house, what to look for outside and inside a house, how to negotiate a good deal, and how to shop for the best mortgage. It even takes you step by step through that confusing process of the settlement closing.

The book is based on straight facts and the authors' years of experience in housing. Coauthor Mike Sumichrast is the Babe Ruth of housing economists, having achieved legendary status as the chief economist of the National Association of Home

Builders. He was in constant demand to testify before Congress, and he met on housing issues with Presidents Nixon, Ford, Carter, Reagan, and Bush.

Mike brings another element to home buying because he is a man who has fought for freedom all of his life. As a soldier in Czechoslovakia, he fought the Nazi invasion of his homeland. When Czechoslovakia fell behind the Iron Curtain, he opposed Communism and escaped in 1948, crossing the Danube River at night in a boat carrying his knapsack and a gun. He went first to Australia, where he began his home-building career, then came to America, where he has become an American success story. Sprinkled throughout this book you will find "Mike's Favorite Stories" passing on his wisdom and humor about his life experiences.

Coauthor Ronald G. Shafer was a reporter and features editor at the *Wall Street Journal* for more than 38 years. For a couple of decades he wrote the popular page 1 column "Washington Wire," specializing in humorous "Minor Memos" at the bottom of the column. It was while he was a Washington reporter covering housing issues that Ron hooked up with Mike Sumichrast for their first housing book.

This time Mike and Ron are joined by Mike's son, Martin Sumichrast. Martin was a schoolboy when the first *Complete Book of Home Buying* was written. Now a successful business-man in Charlotte, North Carolina, he provided research to update this book with an eye to the younger generation of home buyers.

Whatever your age, *The New Complete Book of Home Buying* will arm you with the information you need in order to invest in and buy the house you really want. The goal is to help you buy a home that not only will put a roof over your head, but also will pay off in the future. The dream of a home of your own is alive and well and still living in America.

CHAPTER 1

Home Sweet Home

Still the Best Investment You Will Ever Make

For most Americans, there's no place like home as an investment. You get a roof over your head, and, if you buy wisely, chances are that your house will go up in value. If you want, you can eventually take your profits and move up to a better home. When you're ready to retire and move to a smaller and cheaper establishment, you can pocket your gain tax-free.

The key is to buy your home as an investment, looking for a location, amenities, and an appeal that will pay off later. This is one reason that homeownership is called the American Dream, and it's the envy of the world.

Housing Prices: Up, Up, and Away!

Over the years, home prices in the United States have gone through the roof. When we wrote the first edition of *The Complete Book of Home Buying* in 1979, the median price of a newly built single-family house was $62,900. The median cost of an existing house was $55,700. (Median means halfway between the highest and the lowest prices.)

Mike's Favorite Russia Story

Georgia, a former Republic of the former Soviet Union, population 5 million, is the size of Maryland and the birthplace of Iosif Vissarionovich Dzhugashvili, known as Stalin. Georgia used to be the home of my son-in-law David Davitaia, who is now working at the University of Maryland. I told him: "Look you must have some interesting stories from Georgia that I could use in my book."

"Like what?" he asked.

"Something that has to with lawyers, taxes, and buying houses."

"Not really. You see, we don't have lawyers, we don't pay taxes, and nobody owns homes."

The moral of the story: They are two to one ahead of us.

We predicted that prices would keep on rising, and we were right. In 2003, the median price for a new home had climbed to $194,100, more than triple the 1979 median and up 87 percent from a median of $104,500 in 1987, when our second edition was written. Median prices for existing homes also nearly tripled from 1979, reaching $170,000, and nearly doubled from 1987's $85,600.

The trend is still up. The median price of a new home is expected to rise to $226,000 by 2005. The price of an existing home is likely to increase to a median of $196,000.

Down through the decades, housing has been not only a way to stay ahead of the Dow Joneses, but also a hedge against inflation (see Table 1-1). About the only exception came in the late 1970s and early 1980s, when inflation rose into double digits and mortgage rates actually climbed above a scary 18 percent.

By the year 2002, real estate was climbing rapidly again, even though the economy and the stock market were going into

Table 1-1   New and Existing Home Prices and Inflation

Year	Inflation (percent)	Price of a New Home	Percent Gain	Price of a Existing Home	Percent Gain
1968	1.6	$24,700	8.8	$20,700	4.0
1969	5.4	25,600	3.6	21,600	4.3
1970	5.9	23,400	−8.4*	23,000	6.5
1971	4.3	25,200	7.7	24,800	7.8
1972	3.3	27,699	9.5	26,700	7.7
1973	6.2	32,500	17.8	28,900	8.2
1974	11.0	35,900	10.5	32,000	10.8
1975	9.1	39,000	9.5	35,300	10.3
1976	5.8	44,200	12.5	38,100	7.9
1977	6.5	48,800	10.4	42,900	12.6
1978	7.7	55,700	14.1	48,700	13.5
1979	11.3	62,900	12.9	55,700	14.4
1980	13.5	64,600	2.7	62,600	11.7
1981	10.3	68,900	6.4	66,400	6.8
1982	6.1	69,300	0.6	67,800	2.1
1983	3.2	75,300	8.7	70,300	3.7
1984	4.3	79,900	6.1	72,400	3.0
1985	3.5	84,300	5.5	75,500	4.3
1986	1.9	92,000	9.1	80,300	6.4
1987	3.6	104,500	13.6	85,600	6.6
1988	4.1	112,500	7.6	89,300	4.3
1989	4.8	120,000	6.7	89,500	4.2
1990	5.4	122,900	2.4	92,000	2.6
1991	4.2	120,000	−2.4	97,100	3.8
1992	3.0	121,500	1.3	99,700	2.7
1993	3.3	126,500	4.1	103,100	3.4
1994	2.6	130,000	2.7	107,200	3.9
1995	2.8	133,900	3.0	110,500	3.1
1996	3.3	140,000	4.6	115,800	4.8

(continued)

3

Table 1-1   (*Continued*)

Year	Inflation (percent)	Price of a New Home	Percent Gain	Price of a Existing Home	Percent Gain
1997	1.7	146,000	4.3	121,800	5.2
1998	1.6	152,500	4.5	128,400	5.4
1999	2.7	161,000	5.6	133,300	3.8
2000	3.4	169,000	5.0	139,000	4.2
2001	1.6	175,200	3.7	147,800	6.3
2002	2.4	187,500	7.0	158,300	7.0
2003	2.5	194,100	3.5	170,000	7.4
E-2004	2.5	210,000	8.2	188,500	10.9
E-2005	2.6	226,000	7.6	196,000	4.0

*Minus in 1970 reflects inexpensive homes built under a federal new home subsidy program. + Inflation: Consumer Price Index. E = authors' estimate.
Source: U.S. Census Bureau, National Association of Realtors.

a dive. In hot housing markets, prices went up far, far beyond the national average.

In the northeastern United States, prices of existing homes jumped 35 percent between 2000 and 2003. In Nassau/Suffolk, New York, prices shot up a whopping 46.2 percent in just 2 years. Out West, prices went up 35.2 percent in San Diego. Between 1998 and 2001, homeowners saw over $2 trillion in house price appreciation, according to Freddie Mac, a federally sponsored mortgage company.

Why Are Home Prices Increasing?

The answer to that question is Housing Economics 101: population growth, less land for new homes, increased costs, inflation, higher incomes, and job growth, to mention some basic factors. All of these are pushing the prices of homes higher and higher.

Another factor is that houses simply are bigger than they used to be. The post–World War II slab, Cape Cod houses with 960 square feet of space that a young Mike Sumichrast started building in the 1950s, are the houses of yesteryear. The average living space of new homes has doubled in the past 30 years, from 1189 square feet to 2320 square feet. People want more space: 65 percent of new homes have two-car garages, and 24 percent have three-car garages or larger. Today's homes have more closets, cabinets, doors, and windows. Long gone are the days when the whole family shared one bathroom. More than 55 percent of today's new homes have two-and-a-half bathrooms, and 36 percent have four.

Another reason new home prices are soaring out of sight is the enormous increase in the cost of land. Fifty years ago the cost of developed land was 12.9 percent of the sales price of a house. That share has nearly doubled; it's now 23.5 percent of the sales

---

Mike's Favorite Swimming Pool Story

One day, when I was building a swimming pool in my backyard in Montgomery County, Maryland, somebody rang the doorbell. I went to see who it was. There stood a disheveled guy looking like a prehistoric man or maybe a biblical prototype, with a long beard and hair down to his shoulders.

"What can I do for you?" I asked.

"I am the inspector," he said

"Inspector of what?" I asked.

"The swimming pool inspector," he replied.

"What the hell do I need a pool inspector for?" I asked, baffled. You may not believe me, but it's true. I had at least twelve inspections on this small, insignificant, lousy hole in the ground.

price, even though the size of a typical lot has remained virtually the same (12,839 square feet versus 12,910 square feet).

Environmental and regulatory costs have also skyrocketed. Some of our best friends are environmentalists, but stiffer requirements add to the bottom line. There is a story that if Moses were leading his people to freedom today, he would probably come to them and say, "I've got some good news and some bad news. The good news is that I'm going to part the Red Sea so that you can escape. The bad news is that first I have to file an Environmental Impact Statement."

The regulations don't stop after you buy a home, as Mike Sumichrast discovered when he put a swimming pool in his backyard.

The changes in cost, purchase price, and size can be seen in a house that Mike helped build in 1954 in Morrisville, Pennsylvania (see Table 1-2).

As Table 1-3 shows, in the 50 years between 1954 and 2003, the median price of a new home increased 13.9 times and the

Table 1-2   Cost of a Home in 1954

Grandview Estates West Trenton Avenue Morrisville, PA	
Price......................	$11,250.00
4 Bedrooms and 2 baths	
Loan: 25 years, F.H.A., 4½ percent	
Down Payment	$ 1,250.00
Mortgage	10,000.00
Price	$11,250.00
Principal and interest, plus MIP	59.63
Taxes	10.36
Fire insurance	1.40
Monthly Payment	$71.39

Mike's Favorite Story about What $11,250 Can Buy Today

One way to look at the increasing market value of homes sold is to compare what people could buy for a given amount of money 50 years ago and what they can buy today. Here I am using the sales price of the first houses I built in the United States in 1954.

1954: Single-family home, four bedrooms, two baths, 960 square feet. To live in.

1981: 16- by 40-foot swimming pool. To swim in.

2003: One room 10 feet by 15 feet, or 153 square feet of space. To sleep in.

Table 1-3   50 Years of Changes in the Prices of Homes and Incomes

Year	Median Price per Square Foot	Median Price for New Homes	Median Price for Existing Homes	Median Household Income
1954	$11.75	$ 14,200	$ 13,300	$ 3,150
1995	$56.80	$133,900	$110,500	$34,076
2003	$70.00	$194,100	$170,000	$47,360
2004e	$72.15	$210,000	$188,500	$49,960

e = estimate. *Note:* The 1954 price per square foot was pretty much in line with the FHA cost of $11.10.
Source: Table 1-1 and U.S. Census Bureau. Cost per square foot in 1954 based on 354 Cape Cod houses of 960 square feet, built by the author.

median price of an existing home increased 12.8 times, while household income increased 15 times. The forecast for 2004 shows a further improvement. This greater increase in income made it possible for more people to buy and resulted in a healthy housing market.

Still Buying After All These Increases

Despite the price increases, home sales in the new millennium have surged, even with an economic downturn and a swooning stock market. In 2003, sales of existing homes hit a record high for the third straight year, rising to 6.1 million. Sales of new homes rose to 1,089,000, also a record for a third consecutive year. The main reason was the lowest interest rates in decades, as low as 3 percent or even less in some areas. Refinancing was also at record levels during this period.

How can people still afford to buy? Incomes and interest rates are probably the most important factors in making the decision to buy a home. Fortunately, median household income has continued to rise as well, making it possible for 6.5 million single-family homes to be purchased annually.

Table 1-4 shows changes in the prices of new and existing homes and in median household incomes going back to 1900. It also shows the ratios of the price of a home to household income. This is a critical calculation in terms of people's ability to qualify for a mortgage when purchasing a home.

Back in 1900, the average household paid nearly 10 times its income for a house. The annual income was $490, the price of a new home was $4881, and the price of an existing home was $4500. That resulted in a median price-income ratio of 9.96 for new homes and 9.18 for existing homes.

Home buyers had to pay an even bigger share of their income during the Great Depression of the 1930s. The peak came in 1934, when people paid a median of 18.3 times their income for housing.

By 1940, this ratio had dropped to 5.07 for new homes and 4.77 for existing houses. The ratio had dropped below 3 years of income by the 1960s, mainly because of declining interest rates. As a result, housing starts hit a then-record 1.6 million in 1963.

The good housing times came to an abrupt halt in the late 1970s and early 1980s, when both home sales and home prices

Table 1-4   Home Prices and Income

Year	Median Home Prices New	Median Home Prices Existing	Median Income	Price-Income Ratio New	Price-Income Ratio Existing
1900	$4,881	$4,500	$490	9.96	9.18
1940	6,588	6,200	1,300	5.07	4.77
1950	9,800	8,900	2,450	4.00	3.63
1960	16,652	15,200	5,620	2.96	3.69
1970	23,400	23,000	9,586	2.96	2.70
1980	64,600	62,200	17,710	3.63	3.51
1990	122,900	92,000	29,943	4.10	3.07
1995	133,900	110,500	34,076	3.93	3.24
2000	169,000	139,800	42,151	4.00	3.32
2001	175,200	147,400	42,228	4.14	3.48
2002	187,600	158,300	44,680	4.20	3.57
2003	194,100	170,000	47,360	4.09	3.58
2004	210,000e	188,500	49,960	4.20	3.77
2005	226,000e	196,000	52,900	4.27	3.71

e = estimated.
Source: Prices: National Association of Realtors; Median household income before taxes, U.S. Census Bureau.

ran into double-digit inflation. Record high mortgage rates pushed monthly payments beyond the reach of many buyers. Mortgage money was so hard to come by that bumper stickers appeared that read, "Have You Hugged Your Mortgage Banker Today?"

In recent years, the affordability ratio has remained steady at just above four times income for new homes and below that level for existing homes. This illustrates that as interest rates drop, people are enticed to buy homes. Those who are already living in homes may well opt for taking equity out of their existing home by refinancing it, then improving the home. All of this adds to the pressure on prices, which shows in the price-income ratios. Figure 1-1 shows the trend in median income.

Figure 1-1 Median Income Displays Strong Growth

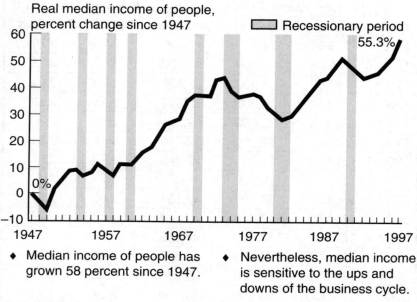

Real median income of people, percent change since 1947

Recessionary period

55.3%

0%

1947   1957   1967   1977   1987   1997

♦ Median income of people has grown 58 percent since 1947.

♦ Nevertheless, median income is sensitive to the ups and downs of the business cycle.

Source: U.S. Census Bureau.

Is a Crash in Housing Prices Coming?

When we wrote *The Complete Book of Home Buying* in 1979, a best-selling book about the coming economic doom recommended that people sell their houses, move into apartments, and invest in collectibles. Another book warned of *The Coming Real Estate Crash*.

In 1980, Dr. Michael Sumichrast was a guest author on NBC's *Today* show along with the author of the real estate crash book. Tom Brokaw co-hosted the show with the late Jessica Savage.

Brokaw told the audience: "I guess the wildest housing market is California. The first home we ever bought was $42,500. I'll never forget it. It took all the money I could scrape up. The lady who sold it to us just sent us a listing the other day, and it sold, very swiftly, for $140,000. No changes in it."

Brokaw then added: "I know a better story. On the beach in California, a house was built for $125,000. A guy thought he made a real killing by selling it for $250,000 in two years. It's now worth $800,000. It's a really small home."

He then asked the guests to give their housing forecasts. The author of the crash book predicted that the average home price would plummet by 50 percent in the coming months. His advice: People would be better off renting than buying.

Mike Sumichrast pounced on this like it was a juicy lamb chop. "To assume a 50 percent drop in the price of homes is to assume a total collapse of the [economic] system, and this is not going to happen. There is no way."

With mortgage rates at 12 percent, Brokaw suggested, maybe people should hold off buying. Sumichrast quickly disagreed: "The best time to buy a house is today, unless you bought it yesterday."

Mike was right on the money, as it turned out. Anybody who sold their house and moved into an apartment to invest in collectibles ended up pouring rent money down the drain and trying to peddle boxes of porcelain dolls at flea markets.

People who bought houses cashed in on the biggest housing boom in U.S. history. Many saw the value of their house soar, enabling them to move up to the house of their dreams. Today, some people are once again predicting a collapse in house prices based on various theories. Our forecast that housing will continue to be a good investment is based on facts.

AFFORDABILITY

Sure, home prices in some costly cities have climbed beyond the reach of the average pocketbook. But overall, incomes have kept pace. Plus, many people can make bigger down payments because of the appreciation of their current houses. That nest egg of savings that helped people buy a first home becomes a golden egg that helps them move up to a costlier one.

Look what has happened since Mike helped build that house in Pennsylvania in the 1950s. The prices of homes sold between 1954 and 2003 increased slightly less than the median household income. People's income determines the price they can afford to pay for a home and the amount of the loan for which they can qualify. If income in a given area is high, the market for real estate tends to be active as long as the vacancy rate is not much above the "normal" vacancy rate.

DEMOGRAPHICS

Driving the housing gains of the past two decades has been the giant post–World War II baby boom generation of more than 70 million people. The boomers will continue to have a huge impact on housing as they age. This is not your father's older generation, ready to stay put in the old homestead or move into a retirement home. When the kids fly the nest, the baby boomers are likely to move up to a bigger house, not down to a smaller one. Many of them are buying town houses or second homes. They will still be buying into old age.

Meanwhile, the baby boomers' kids are now coming of home-buying age. These "echo-boom" children are marrying and having children. Having seen their parents prosper through home ownership, they want a dream home of their own.

In addition, there are just a lot more people. The 2000 census showed that there were 281.4 million people living in the United States, a gain of 23.7 million in just 10 years. By the year 2010, the population will reach as many as 310 million. And you thought it was crowded now.

Population increases put strong pressure on the supply of homes—people simply have to live somewhere. To accommodate nearly 2½ million additional bodies every year, we need to build more homes. Thus, our production of new homes runs between 1.5 million and 1.7 million units annually.

As their needs change, people will want to move from their current apartments or houses. Those with growing children are

likely to look for a larger home. Older people may look for condominiums or town houses. This is the reason that we resell
over 5.5 million existing homes each year.

GIMME SHELTER

Taxes are another reason that people will keep buying houses. A
home of your own provides about the only substantial tax
deductions that the average person can claim. The interest you
pay on your mortgage is fully deductible from your federal,
state, and local income taxes. That pushes down the net cost of
your mortgage payment.

You may hate to pay property taxes, but the good news is
that these taxes, too, are deductible. The lender usually collects
these taxes as part of your monthly payment and pays them
when they come due.

What's more, with changes in the law that were made in
the 1990s, most home buyers will never have to pay taxes on the
profits they reap each time they sell their homes. The law
exempts a gain of up to $500,000 for couples and $250,000 for
individuals who have owned their house for at least two years.

In other words, housing is an investment that keeps on giving. A home of your own has become like a giant piggy bank.
Because of price appreciation, your house is storing up investment appreciation. Meanwhile, you get a hefty tax deduction.
And you can tap this piggy bank for major needs, such as home
improvements or college tuition. Finally, you can cash in your
profits if you decide to move to a cheaper house.

FOLLOW THE DREAM

Another factor driving demand is the American dream of home
ownership. Today a record 68 percent of Americans own their
own homes, up from 64.1 percent 10 years ago and 42 percent
in 1940. More than 80 percent of older Americans own their
homes, but the biggest gain in the past decade has been among
people under age 25 (see Table 1-5).

Table 1-5 Home Ownership Rates by Age of Householder

Age Group	1982	1992	2002
Under 25	19.3%	14.9%	23.0%
25–29	38.6	33.6	39.0
30–34	57.1	50.5	55.0
35–39	67.6	61.4	65.2
40–44	73.0	69.1	71.7
45–49	76.0	74.2	74.9
50–54	78.8	76.2	77.8
55–59	80.0	79.3	80.8
60–64	80.1	81.2	81.5
65–69	77.9	80.8	82.8
70–74	75.2	79.0	82.5
75 and up	71.0	73.3	78.4

Source: U.S. Census Bureau.

Minority and immigrant households lag behind in home ownership, which opens up a big area for further growth.

IMMIGRATION

Another push for home buying comes from immigrants. The United States gets about 850,000 immigrants each year. And that's just the ones that we count. The number coming to the United States illegally is simply huge. An article in *Free Republic* with the title "Movers and Shakers" estimates that between 3 million and 5 million illegal migrants entered the United States between 1992 and 1999. This is an additional 428,000 to 714,000 people each year.

As a result of these population changes, "We expect demographic forces to continue to drive housing demand for the rest of the decade," said David Berson, chief economist at Fannie Mae, the big secondary-mortgage company.

Whether they come from Europe or Ecuador, immigrants see a home of their own as a major part of the Great American

Dream. Just ask Vojtech and Olga Kebis, who came to the United States in the late 1980s from what was then Czechoslovakia with two small children and almost nothing else.

The young couple saved every penny they could. Within 2 years, they were able to buy their first home—a $97,000 town house in Springfield, Virginia, a suburb of Washington, D.C. That same year they also paid for Vojtech's parents to visit from Czechoslovakia, which at that time was behind the Iron Curtain, where few people could own their own homes.

"When I heard that my boy was thinking about buying a house, my reaction was that this is nothing but a bunch of American propaganda," the elder Mr. Kebis said after he came to visit. "But now I can see that it was not."

It was no propaganda. Today the Kebises' $97,000 town house is worth a cool $320,000.

Ten Biggest Home-Buying Mistakes

As you embark on your home-buying adventure, here is a list of 10 home-buying mistakes that you should keep in mind, whether you are buying a newly built home or an existing one. The advice comes from David Weekley, CEO of David Weekley Homes in Houston, Texas.

Not doing your homework. Knowledge is power. A tremendous amount of information is available on the Internet. There is no excuse for entering the market unprepared.

Trying to make a shrewd investment. People need to buy based on what fits their family. Don't try to guess what will happen to the market.

Choosing a poor location. Even within a neighborhood, location matters. Is the home on the busiest street? Is there a shopping center out the back window?

Overlooking an inferior floor plan because of an attractive exterior. The house may have gorgeous curb appeal, but you don't live on the lawn. No matter how attractive the exterior, you need a livable home.

Overlooking how the house will function for your family. How do you really live? Do you really need a formal dining room and living room? Would you be happier with an eat-in kitchen and a great room and a den to use as a home office? The house needs to fit only one family—yours.

Not having an existing home properly inspected. This is not the time for surprises. Get an inspection by a qualified, respected professional.

Not checking out the builder's reputation on a new home. Talk to three or four people who live in the builder's homes and see what they have to say. If one builder did all the houses in a neighborhood, talk to the residents and get their input. (This is also a great way to see what your neighbors would be like.)

Not getting what you want because you're impatient. This is a big decision. You need time. Impatient decisions can lead to mistakes.

Waiting for a better market and interest rates. As Warren Buffett says, the rearview mirror is always clearer than the windshield.

Not buying at all. If you can afford a home and you don't make that purchase, you'll lose the benefit of tax deductions, growing home equity, and the appreciation in value

A Home Is More than an Investment

Housing markets (and stock markets) run hot and cold. But over the years, housing as an investment has compared favorably with other investments ranging from stocks and bonds to gold and pork bellies. Moreover, in terms of the return on your investment, the gains from housing are usually higher than you are sometimes led to believe.

News reports, for example, will say that between 2000 and 2002, prices of new homes rose at a level of 5.3 percent annually and prices of existing homes rose 6.6 percent annually, somewhat more than you could get—deducting inflation—on a good solid investment. The comparison might be accurate if you paid cash for your home, which only about 3 percent of buyers of single-family homes do.

The return on your investment, however, is based on your investment in your home, not on its total price. If, for example, you paid the current average price of $200,000 for a new single-family home and made a 20 percent down payment, your investment is $40,000. If the value goes up only 5 percent in 1 year, to $210,000, you have "earned" $10,000. But the return on your investment is much higher than 5 percent. A $10,000 gain on a $40,000 investment is 25 percent, which you can't beat many places. And for many homeowners, the gains have been much higher.

But investing in a home has benefits beyond those provided by investments in stocks and pork bellies. You can't live in pork bellies. A home is a good investment because you can live in it. It's a place you can truly call your own—a place where you can pound nails into the wall if you want to, a place where you can invite your friends or where you can be alone, a place where you can raise your family or entertain your grandchildren.

Mike's Favorite Little-Boy Story

In July 2003 my son Michael visited me at my house in Potomac, Maryland, with his four children. His 8-year-old boy Ryan came to my wife, Eva, and said: "This is a children's dream house. You have a swimming pool with a slide, a basketball court, a Jacuzzi, two dogs, and a huge master bedroom I can run in."

That is the stuff that dream homes are really made of.

CHAPTER 2

Holy Home Prices, or What Can You Afford?

You may think that home prices are climbing beyond anything you can afford. In some places, that's true. In Beverly Hills in 2003, "Material Girl" Madonna bought a French Regency design home on Sunset Boulevard, complete with a tennis court, for $13 million. In the Washington, D.C., suburb of McLean, Virginia, Ethel and Robert F. Kennedy's estate went on the block for a cool $25 million.

Actually, though, there are plenty of houses out there that can fit your pocketbook. In fact, you may be able to afford a costlier house than you think. After all, despite all the price increases, half of all homes sold in the United States each year sell for under $200,000.

The rule of thumb is that you can afford to pay 2.5 times your annual income. Thus, if your household income is $50,000 a year, you can afford to buy a $125,000 home. If your gross income is $75,000, you can afford to buy a $187,500 house. But the rule of thumb about rule of thumbs is that they don't tell the whole story.

What you can afford depends on your individual situation. Are you a first-time buyer, or do you own a home already? Do you have a lot of savings or profit from your first home with which to make a sizable down payment, or do you need a mortgage with a very small down payment? Do you owe just a little money, or are your credit card bills approaching the national debt?

The 28 Percent Rule

Let's start with the basics. Typically lenders will require your monthly mortgage payment to be no more than 28 percent of your monthly income. Sometimes that can be expanded to 29 or 30 percent. For a Federal Housing Administration (FHA) loan, the maximum is 31 percent, and for a Veterans Administration (VA) mortgage, it can go up to 40 percent.

Let us assume that a lender calculates your ability to pay using a 28 percent rule. Table 2-1 shows the income needed to qualify for mortgages of various sizes. Your monthly payment actually consists of four parts, called PITI—principal and interest on your mortgage, property taxes, and insurance.

But every home buyer is different. You can get a quick and dirty calculation of what you can afford by clicking on one of the hundreds of real estate web sites and using an affordability calculator. Consider, for example, the site for Fannie Mae, a private mortgage company sponsored by the federal government, at www.homepath.com. On the Home page, click on "Homepath" and look in the text for "mortgage calculators." Click on that, and on the next page you will see "How Much House Can You Afford?" Type in your income, your monthly debt, the funds you have for a down payment, a mortgage interest range, the length of the loan, and what percentage of the purchase price you are putting down. Click the button and voilà, you have a price range that fits your income.

Table 2-1 Match Your Income to Your Mortgage Payments

Price	Percentage Down Payment	Mortgage Amount	Mortgage Payment	Income Needed at 28 Percent
$100,000	10%	$90,000	$924	$39,600
$100,000	20%	$80,000	$917	$39,300
$150,000	10%	$135,000	$1,386	$59,400
$150,000	20%	$120,000	$1,372	$58,800
$170,000	10%	$153,000	$1,571	$63,329
$170,000	20%	$136,000	$1,554	$62,600

Note: Mortgage payment includes principal and interest on a conventionally financed 30-year mortgage at a rate of 5.875 percent, property taxes, and home insurance. The information provided here is only an estimate.

Mike's Favorite Affordability Story

In 1967, my wife, Marika, suggested that we should move from our home in Bethesda, Maryland, near Washington, D.C, to a bigger house farther out, in Potomac, Maryland, that cost $50,250. As a housing expert, I thought that was too much to pay. The $350 monthly payment would be nearly double what we were paying for the Bethesda house, which we had bought for $27,000 in 1963. Marika insisted that the house would be a good investment, and she was right. Even before a major remodeling in 1986, the value had soared to more than $400,000. Today the house is worth more than $950,000.

For example, if you have an annual income of about $50,000, depending on the mortgage rate, you can afford a house selling for about $110,000 to $118,000 (see Table 2-2).

With a little planning, you can afford more house than you thought you could.

Table 2-2 How Much House Can You Afford?

FANNIE MAE

Gross income:*
(Pretax income)

$ [50,000] [Worksheet]

[Yearly ▼]

Monthly debt:*
(Do not include debt that will be
paid off within the next 6 months)

$ [600] [Worksheet]

**Funds available for down payment
& closing costs:***

$ [20000] [Worksheet]

Interest rate range:*
(Minimum and maximum interest
rates; maximum range equals 2%)

[5.5] %

from

[6.5] %

to

Mortgage term:
(Length of the mortgage)

[30]

[Years ▼]

Down payment percentage:

[10] % of sales price

Closing cost percentage:
(Includes origination fees, discount
points, and other closing costs)

[5] % of sales price

Monthly taxes & insurance:
(Includes property, hazard, flood,
and mortgage insurance)

[0.25] % of sales price

Information You Entered

Monthly Income	**$4,166.67**
Monthly Debt	**$600.00**
Available Funds	**$20,000.00**
Results	
Monthly Payment You Can Afford	**$900.00**

Table 2-2 (Continued)

Interest Rate	Sales Price	Loan Amount	Monthly Payment	Down Payment & Closing Costs	Funds Surplus
5.500%	$118,263.86	$106,437.48	$900.00	$17,739.58	$2,260.42
5.625%	$117,173.65	$105,456.29	$900.00	$17,576.04	$2,423.96
5.750%	$116,096.74	$104,487.07	$900.00	$17,414.51	$2,585.49
5.875%	$115,033.03	$103,529.73	$900.00	$17,254.95	$2,745.05
6.000%	$113,982.41	$102,584.17	$900.00	$17,097.36	$2,902.64
6.125%	$112,944.79	$101,650.31	$900.00	$16,941.72	$3,058.28
6.250%	$111,920.04	$100,728.04	$900.00	$16,788.00	$3,212.00
6.375%	$110,908.06	$99,817.26	$900.00	$16,636.21	$3,363.79
6.500%	$109,908.73	$98,917.86	$900.00	$16,486.31	$3,513.69

Source: www.Homepath.com. HomePath® is a registered trademark of Fannie Mae.

Down Payments: Why Size Matters

If you can make a bigger down payment, you may get more housing bang for your bucks. The traditional down payment ranges from zero or 3 percent to 20 percent of the purchase price. But the more you put down up front, the more you can pay for a house while keeping the monthly payment within reach of your pocketbook. Some people put down 25 percent, 30 percent, or more. They may be able to get a lower mortgage rate by doing so. Often, they already own a house and can use the appreciation from the sale to put more down on the house they buy.

Look how it works in the example in Table 2-3. If you can afford a monthly payment of about $950 and you put 10 percent

Table 2-3   Bigger Down Payment, More House

Monthly Housing Expenses $943		Monthly Housing Expenses $1333	
Down Payment	House Price	Down Payment	House Price
5%	$120,000	5%	$170,000
10%	$130,000	10%	$180,000
15%	$138,000	15%	$195,000
20%	$145,000	20%	$210,000
25%	$160,000	25%	$225,000

Note: Monthly housing expenses are the average of all five price ranges, they varied from $916 to $963, for an average of $943, and from $1315 to $1354, for an average of $1333.

Calculation assumes a 30-year mortgage at 6 percent, 2 points, 0.78 percent insurance, 3 percent closing costs and 1.1825 percent annual property taxes. In a real-life case, the lender would very probably charge more points and a higher interest rate, as well as requiring private mortgage insurance, for buyers with less than 20 percent down. However the basic principle of lowering your monthly housing cost with a higher down payment is very sound.

down, you will be able to pay $130,000 for a house. But if you put 25 percent down, you can afford to buy a $160,000 house with the same monthly payment.

BRINGING DOWN THE HOUSE PAYMENT

Another option is to use a bigger down payment to lower your monthly payments. Consider a $170,000 home with a 5.875 percent mortgage for 30 years. With a 20 percent down payment, the monthly mortgage payment is $1,077. But with a 30 percent down payment, it drops to $985. And with 35 percent down, the payment is $917. (See Table 2-4.)

So if you can beg, borrow, or steal down payment money, you may be better off. (Well, don't really steal it, or you may end up in the Big House. There are plenty of legal sources for the cash.)

Table 2-4 Shrinking the Monthly Payment
Home sales price: $170,000. Conventional loan at 5.875% for 30 years

LTV Ratio	Down Payment	Monthly Payment	Loan Amount
17.6%	$30,000	$1,119	$145,000
20.0%	$34,000	$1,077	$141,904
23.6%	$40,000	$1,052	$135,765
29.4%	$50,000	$985	$125,534
35.3%	$60,000	$917	$115,302
41.2%	$70,000	$850	$105,071
50.0%	$85,000	$750	$89,724

LTV = loan to value.

Source: www.ginniemae.gov.

ALLOWABLE SOURCES FOR A DOWN PAYMENT

You can't just take out another loan to make the down payment on your home loan. Here's the official word about down payments from the U.S. Department of Housing and Urban Development's Ginne Mae housing finance agency on where you are allowed to get the cash.

> *Co-Borrower*—Income or additional funds from a spouse may provide additional funds to support the down payment costs. You also may want to consider whether a roommate or co-dweller may relieve the financial burden.
>
> *Gifts*—Monetary gifts from family members can support your down payment requirements since no funds repayment is required.
>
> *Inheritance/Trust Funds*—Inherited money from family members or a trust fund are also acceptable sources of down payment since no fund repayment is required.

Borrowing/loan—Monetary support from friends or relatives can be a solution.

Retirement Funds—Some retirement funds like the 401K plans may allow you to borrow a certain percentage from your retirement fund. You should check with your local lenders to see if they allow home buyers to borrow against their retirement funds. Note: Borrowing against your 401K plan requires that you repay the amount; therefore, when lenders calculate your loan qualifications, they will add your 401K repayments in calculating your monthly payments.

Source: www.ginniemae.gov

Keep an Eye on Interest Rates

How much house you can afford to buy depends on your income, the down payment, the mortgage rate, and the length of the mortgage, but it also depends on interest rates. During the early 2000s, the price of the home that a typical family could afford went up because interest rates went down. If interest rates go up, what you can afford goes down.

The National Association of Realtors publishes a monthly Housing Affordability Index, based on a 25 percent qualifying ratio for monthly housing expenses to gross monthly income and a 20 percent down payment. The index measures whether a typical family can qualify for a mortgage loan on a typical home. An index above 100 indicates that a family earning the median income has more than enough income to qualify for a mortgage loan on a median-priced home. The Housing Affordability Index increased sharply in 2003 to 140.5 from 129.2 in 2000 (see Table 2-5).

A decline in interest rates in 2003 increased the ability of median-income home buyers to purchase homes at the median

Table 2-5 The National Association of Realtors Housing Affordability Index

Year	Median Price of a Single-Family Home	Mortgage Rate	Monthly P&I Payment	Payment as a Percent of Family Income	Median Income	Qualifying Income	Index
2000	$139,000	8.03	$818	19.3%	$50,732	$39,264	129.2
2001	$147,800	7.03	$789	18.4%	$51,407	$37,872	135.0
2002	$158,200	6.55	$804	18.3%	$52,692	$38,592	136.5
2003	$170,000	5.842	$793	17.8%	$53,463	$38,064	140.5

Source: National Association of Realtors, www.realtor.org.

Table 2-6 Figuring Your Monthly Payment
Monthly Payments Table per $1000 Borrowed

Interest Rate	15 Years	20 Years	30 Years
5.00%	$7.91	$6.60	$5.37
5.50	8.17	6.88	5.68
6.00	8.44	7.16	6.00
6.50	8.71	7.46	6.32
7.00	8.99	7.75	6.65
7.50	9.27	8.06	6.99
8.00	9.56	8.36	7.34
8.50	9.85	8.68	7.69
9.00	10.14	9.00	8.05
9.50	10.44	9.32	8.41
10.00	10.75	9.65	8.78
10.50	11.06	9.99	9.15
11.00	11.37	10.32	9.52
11.50	11.69	10.66	9.90
12.00	12.01	11.01	10.29

price of $170,000, or $31,000 more than the $139,000 house they could afford in 2000. The qualifying income fell to $38,064 from $39,264 in 2000.

You can calculate what your payments will be online at the numerous real estate web sites mentioned in a later chapter. Or, if you prefer the old-fashioned way, you can do it with pencil and paper, using Table 2-6.

From Table 2-6, the payments on a 6 percent loan of $150,000 for 30 years would be $6.00 × 150 = $900 principal and interest. To figure your total payments, add an estimated 1.5 percent of the value of your home for property taxes ($150,000 × 1.5 percent = $225) and your estimated home-owners' insurance premium, let us say, $40 per month.

The final result would look like this:

Monthly principal and interest	$900
Monthly property tax payment	225
Monthly insurance payment	40
Total monthly payment	$1165

Shrink That Debt!

How much money you owe has a big impact on how big a mortgage you can get. Lenders generally require that your mortgage payment and other long-term debt not exceed 36 percent of your income. So the lower your debt, the more you can put toward your new house.

Consider, for instance, a household in Frederick, Maryland, with $50,000 annual income and monthly debt payments of $250. With a down payment of $24,389 and a mortgage rate of 5.875 percent, this family can afford to pay $189,614 for a house. A second family with the same income and $700 in monthly debt payments can only afford to buy a house for $125,619 (see Table 2-7).

Table 2-7   What an Income of $50,000 Can
Buy with Variation in Monthly Debt
(Conventionally financed 5.875% 30-year mortgage loan)

Monthly Debt				Maximum Sale Price	Loan Amount
Credit Cards	Car Payments	Others*	Total		
$0	$0	$0	$0	$195,539	$166,208
$0	$250	$0	$250	$189,614	$161,172
$0	$500	$0	$500	$154,061	$130,952
$200	$400	$100	$700	$125,619	$106,776
$250	$500	$250	$1,000	$82,956	$70,513

*Child support, alimony, student loan.
Source: www.ginniemae.gov.

Cut down on your debt before you apply for a mortgage. Get rid of those nasty credit card and car payments. It's better to suffer some pain now, so that soon you can enjoy the pleasure of buying the house you want.

Property Taxes:
The Good, the Bad, and the Deductible

In most cases, you pay your property taxes as a part of your mortgage payment, and the mortgage lender sends your payments to the local tax collector's office. You can find out what the property taxes on a house are from the seller, or you can check local government records. Many localities now put tax payments and tax rates online.

Property taxes are based on the assessed value of the house and your local tax rate of so much per $100 of assessed value. In most localities, the property tax is changed every year—and it almost always goes up. Property taxes vary widely by location. Table 2-8 gives a few examples of high and low rates.

HOMEOWNER TAX BREAKS

The good news is that property taxes, along with the interest payments on your mortgage, are deductible on your federal, state, and local income taxes. In the early years of a mortgage, almost all of your payment goes toward interest rather than principal. This is the only remaining tax shelter for average Americans, and it adds up to more than $60 billion a year.

Consider the tax savings on a house in Prince George's County, Maryland, with a $100,000 mortgage at 7 percent interest for 30 years. In the first year, the savings range from $1,470 for somebody in the 15 percent tax bracket to $3,234 for somebody in the 33 percent tax bracket (see Table 2-9).

Good news on taxes is hard to find, so you should take it when you get it, as Mike Sumichrast once discovered.

Table 2-8 High and Low Property Tax Areas

State/Province	Lowest Locations	Real Estate Tax	State/Province	Highest Locations	Real Estate Tax
AL	Montgomery	$478	NY	Manhattan	$11,738
LA	La Place	$520	CA	San Jose	$9,107
LA	Ruston	$525	CA	San Francisco	$9,004
AL	Decatur	$603	NJ	Princeton	$8,508
LA	Monroe	$710	NY	New City	$8,499
AL	Mobile	$740	NY	New York City B	$8,038
SC	Florence	$762	NJ	Flemington	$7,386
SC	Hartsville	$776	NJ	Hunterdon County	$7,386
DE	Seaford	$822	NJ	Wayne	$7,203
AL	Tuscaloosa	$829	CA	Thousand Oaks	$6,743
AL	Huntsville	$836	MI	Ann Arbor	$6,617
TN	New Johnsonville	$903	CA	San Luis Obispo	$6,476
TN	Waverly	$903	FL	Miami	$6,425
LA	Lake Charles	$905	IL	Chicago	$6,355
LA	New Orleans	$929	CA	San Diego	$6,328
SC	Charleston	$939	CA	Los Angeles	$6,273
LA	Baton Rouge	$1,002	NJ	Deepwater	$6,087

The table(s) represents the annual real estate taxes on a 2200-square-foot home.

Source: Runzheimer International.

Table 2-9 Homeowner Tax Savings

Actual Monthly Payments after Income Tax Deductions	
7% 30-year conventional loan	
Purchase price of home	$125,000
Cash	$ 25,000
Loan	$100,000
Monthly payments, principal and interest	$882
Monthly property taxes	$236
Monthly insurance	$40
Total monthly payments	$1,158
First-year expenses for tax purposes:	
Monthly interest payment	$6,967
Monthly property taxes	$2,832
Total tax deduction	$9,799
33% tax bracket savings—first year	$3,234
28% tax bracket savings—first year	$2,744
15% tax bracket savings—first year	$1,470
(To calculate deduction, multiply tax bracket by total tax deductions)	
Total monthly cost, first year = $1,123 × 12	$13,896
Minus tax deduction (28% tax bracket)	2,744
Actual annual costs	$11,152

Note: Assuming the house will be sold in 7 years, this is the annual maximum tax savings: Maximum first-year annual tax savings: $3787, second year $3379, third year $3349, fourth year $3317, fifth year $3283, sixth year $3246, and seventh year $3207, for a total of $23,568.

Source: Your Path to Homeownership, www.GinnieMae.com.

Mike's Favorite Tax Story

I once tried to personally help reduce the national debt, but I didn't get very far. It happened like this:

I was called into the Internal Revenue Service to be audited. I prepared myself well with all the documents, receipts, checks, and so forth. My accountant could not make the meeting, so I went alone. After about 2 hours, the IRS lady who did the audit came back and gave me the news: "Actually, we owe you $324.52."

"Why don't you keep it?" I said. "America has done so much for me. Our government needs the money more than I do."

"That's nice of you," she replied, "but I don't know how to do that. Let me check with my superior."

She came back in about 5 minutes. "My superior said that we cannot accept your money."

"And why not, if I may ask?"

"Well, he said that it would mess up the IRS book-keeping."

Shopping for Homeowner's Insurance

The fourth part of your PITI is insurance. The lender will require that you buy a policy to insure your home against fire and damage. You pay for the insurance every month as part of your monthly mortgage payments. The mortgage company will add the cost into your monthly payment and hold your payments in escrow until the insurance is due. But the policy is *your* responsibility—from the company you choose to the types of coverage you select. If your mortgage holder chose for you, you should find out the details immediately, then compare.

Six Steps to Saving on Insurance

1. *Shop around for the best price.*
2. *Raise your deductible.* Deductibles are the amount of money you have to pay toward a loss before your insurance company starts to pay a claim, according to the terms of your policy. The higher your deductible, the more money you can save on your premiums. Nowadays, most insurance companies recommend a deductible of at least $500. If you can afford to raise your deductible to $1,000, you may save as much as 25 percent.
3. *Buy your home and auto policies from the same insurer.*
4. *Improve your home security.* You can get a discount if your house has a home security system.
5. *Stay with the same insurer you had on a previous house.* They may give you a break to keep you.
6. *Consider the location and features of your house when you buy.* You may pay less for insurance if you buy a house close to a fire hydrant or in a community that has a professional rather than a volunteer fire department. It may also be cheaper if your home's electrical, heating and plumbing systems are less than 10 years old.

Source: U.S. General Services Administration—Insurance Information Institute.

Still More Costs to Think About

PRIVATE MORTGAGE INSURANCE

If you make less than a 20 percent down payment, you will have to get private mortgage insurance (PMI) on the amount by which your equity—the part that you own—is under 20 percent. The cost varies from lender to lender. But here is an example: On a 30-year loan with 17.6 percent down, some lenders require an up-front cash payment at closing, typically 0.4 percent of the loan amount, to cover the first year. On a $145,996 loan, 0.4 percent will mean $584. In subsequent years, the PMI renewal premiums on the same loan can range from $400 to $450 and are paid as part of your monthly payments. Other lenders include PMI in the monthly payments from the beginning.

Remember that when your equity in the home reaches 20 percent through your repayments plus the home's appreciation in value, these payments should, in theory, stop. If the homeowner doesn't shout loudly, they often don't.

CLOSING COSTS

When a house sale is closed, everybody has to pay closing costs. These consist of "points" that the lender charges (a point is equal to 1 percent of the mortgage amount), advance tax and insurance payments, title insurance, and other charges. We discuss these in detail in a later chapter. Usually they amount to 3 to 7 percent of the mortgage.

MOVING COSTS

Finally, you need to make sure that you have some money left over to pay the movers, or at least to rent a truck to cart your belongings to your new house. You probably will also want to buy some new furniture, some draperies, and other things for the new house.

A Home-Buying Worksheet

To determine how much you personally can afford to pay for a house, the best thing to do is to sit down and do a personal financial accounting of what you make, what you owe, and what you really can afford. You can find plenty of worksheets on real estate sites on the Internet. Table 2-10 is a sample worksheet to get you started.

TABLE 2-10 What Can You Afford?

1. How Much Money Do You Make?		
Income:	Borrower	Co-borrower
Base salary (gross less taxes	$_____	$_____
Overtime.	_____	_____
Commissions (less expenses)	_____	_____
Bonus	_____	_____
Dividends	_____	_____
Interest	_____	_____
Nontaxable income (describe)		
	_____	_____
Other income (must have a remaining term of at least 3 years):		
Notes receivable	_____	_____
Child support	_____	_____
Alimony	_____	_____
Investment income	_____	_____
Pensions _____	_____	_____
Other income (describe)	_____	_____
Net Average Income	$_____	_____
Total Income(s)	$_____	_____

2. What Are Your Average Monthly Nonhousing Expenses?

Food and household supplies	$_____
Clothing	_____
Medical costs	_____
Life and casualty insurance	_____
Automobile, including insurance	_____
Education	_____
Commuting	_____
Recreation, hobbies	_____
Interest charges on credit cards	_____
Installment payments	_____
Child support	_____
Alimony	_____

TABLE 2-10 (*Continued*)

Telephone... _____
Dues, fees.. _____
Cleaning, hair, other personal expenses........... _____
Travel... _____
Other miscellaneous expenses......................... _____
Savings... _____
Investment.. _____
    Total Average Nonhousing Expenses...........$_____

3. Your Monthly Income Available for Housing:
Net average income (total from 1)................. $_____
Subtract monthly nonhousing expenses
(total from 2)... _____
    Monthly Income Available for
    Housing Expenses.................................. $_____

4. Average Monthly Housing Expenses (house you are considering buying):
Monthly mortgage payment......................... $_____
Condominium fees (maintenance,
recreation, etc.).. _____
Property taxes.. _____
Utilities (gas, electric, oil, water, garbage)........... _____
Personal property liability insurance................. _____
Other monthly expenses (repairs,
maintenance, etc.)....................................... _____
    Average Monthly Housing Expenses.......... $_____

5. How Much Down Payment Can You Afford?
    Available Funds:

Liquid assets
Bank accounts.. $_____
Savings and loan accounts........................... _____
Stocks—liquid assets held by broker............... _____
Bonds .... _____
Mutual funds.. _____

(continued)

TABLE 2-10 (*Continued*)

Savings certificates ...._____
Gift(s) ...._____
Life insurance (cash surrender value) ...._____
Vested in retirement funds..........._____
Other liquid assets (except real estate)........_____
    Total Available Liquid Assets ...._____
Subtract amount you must keep in reserve........_____
    Actual Usable Liquid Assets ...._____

6. Cash Expenses Needed to Buy a House:
Cash for closing costs...........................$_____
Moving expenses ...._____
Furniture, etc. ...._____
Other expected expenses ...._____
    Total Expected Expenses ...._____

7. What You Can Afford to Spend on Down Payment:
Total available funds (from 5) ....$_____
Minus total expected expenses (from 6) ...$_____
    Equals amount you can spend on
    down payment ....$_____

8. Amount of Mortgage Needed:
Sales price of the house ....$_____
Minus down payment you can
afford (from 7) ....$_____
Equals mortgage you will need to finance ..$_____

To Rent or to Buy? That Is the Question

Our view is that if you can afford it, buying is almost always better. The only exception is if you live in an area where rents are unusually low. Even then, you still are probably better off building equity in your own home.

Is renting less costly than buying? In most cases, the answer is clearly no! These are the main reasons:

Even if your monthly rent for an apartment is lower now than the monthly payment for a house, that's not the whole story. For one thing, you can be absolutely sure that your rent will go up, whereas your mortgage payment will stay relatively stable. Meanwhile, as the owner of a house, you have the right to tax deductions for your mortgage interest payments and property taxes. Over the longer term, you save a tremendous amount of money by buying rather than renting, since your home will appreciate in value, whereas renting will let you save nothing but rent receipts. This is one of the few ways in which average people can accumulate wealth. You will have privacy, and you can even get a dog if you want to without a landlord telling you no pets.

Table 2-11 gives the pros and cons of renting and buying.

Table 2-12 is a chart from the Department of Housing and Urban Development to help you decide. You can plug in your own numbers by going to the HUD web site at www.hud.com.

Where You Live Makes a Difference

How much home you get for your money depends on where you want to live. Typical home prices vary widely across the country. Three houses tell the story. In Florissant, Missouri, near St. Louis, you can get a three-bedroom, two-bath home with 1602 square feet for $175,000.

In the high-priced Los Angeles area, $175,000 buys you a two-bedroom house in Lynwood, California, with one bath and only 1082 square feet.

But in low-priced Rochester, New York, for $175,000 you can get a four-bedroom, two-and-a-half-bath home with a two-car garage and 2060 square feet of living space.

Overall, as Table 2-13 shows, housing is most costly in the western United States, where the median price in 2003 was $238,000. The cheapest region was the Midwest, where the median home price was $142,000. Those regional differences can have a huge impact on what you can afford.

Table 2-11   Buy versus Rent Comparison Chart

	Advantages	Disadvantages
Buy	Property builds equity	Responsible for maintenance
	Sense of community, stability, and security	Responsible for property taxes
	Free to change decor and landscaping	Possibility of foreclosure and loss of equity
	Not dependent on landlord to maintain property	Less mobility than renting
Rent	Little or no responsibility for maintenance	No tax benefits
	Easier to move	No equity is built up
		No control over rent increases
		Possibility of eviction

Source: www.hud.gov.

Table 2-12   Buying versus Renting

● Current Rent:	$750
● Purchase Price of Home:	$150,000
● Percentage of Down Payment:	10%
● Length of Loan Term (years):	30
● Interest Rate:	7.5%
● Years You Plan to Stay in This Home:	10
● Yearly Property Tax Rate:	1%
● Yearly Home Value Increase Rate:	2%

Result Returned:	Rent	Buy
Price of Home After Appreciation:		$182,849
Remaining Balance After 10 Years:		$117,340
Equity Earned:		$65,509
Tax Savings (at 28%):		$32,549
Avg. Monthly Payment Over Time:	$834	$550
Total Payment:	$100,080	$66,017
Total Savings On:	Buying: $34,063	

Source: www.hud.com.

California clearly has the highest-priced housing in the country. No place tops San Francisco, where the median price for an existing home has soared by 25 percent, from $454,600 in 2000 to $568,200 in 2003. Prices in the second highest-priced area, Orange County, California, skyrocketed even more, rising 61.5 percent, from $316,000 in 2000 to $510,800 in 2003. San Diego ranked third, while Boston was fourth with a median price of $432,700 in 2003 (see Table 2-14).

Table 2-13 Income Needed to Buy a Median-Priced Home with 10% Down Payment, by Regions

	Northeast	Midwest	South	West
Purchase Price	$197,000	$142,000	$158,000	$238,000
Cash: Down payment	$ 19,700	$ 14,200	$ 15,800	$ 23,800
Points	$ 922	$ 665	$ 739	$ 1,114
Closing costs	$ 5,910	$ 4,620	$ 4,740	$ 7,140
Total cash required	$ 26,532	$ 19,125	$ 21,279	$ 32,054
Monthly debt permitted	$ 403	$ 291	$ 323	$ 487
Loan amount	$177,300	$127,800	$142,200	$214,200
Monthly housing expenses	$ 1,411	$ 1,017	$ 1,132	$ 1,705
Mortgage payment	$ 1,035	$ 746	$ 830	$ 1,250
Taxes and insurance	$ 300	$ 216	$ 240	$ 362
Mortgage insurance	$ 77	$ 55	$ 62	$ 93
Monthly income required	$ 5,040	$ 3,633	$ 4,042	$ 6,089
Annual income required	$ 60,480	$ 43,596	$ 48,504	$ 73,068
Compare this with income required with 20% and 5% down payment				
20% down payment	$ 52,250	$ 37,668	$ 41,916	$ 63,132
5% down payment	$ 64,860	$ 46,752	$ 52,070	$ 78,360

Note: Purchase price of home is the median price of existing homes in October 2003. Conventional mortgage is for 30 years, with 0.52 point and a 5.57% annual interest rate. Based on 28% ratio of monthly expenses to income.

Table 2-14 The 10 Costliest Housing Areas—Existing Homes Sold

Area	Median Sales Price				
	2000	**2001**	**2002**	**2003***	**2000–2003**
1. San Francisco, CA	$454,600	$475,900	$517,100	$568,200	25.0%
2. Orange County, CA	$316,200	$355,600	$412,700	$510,800	61.5
3. San Diego, CA	$269,400	$298,600	$364,200	$436,500	47.3
4. Boston, MA	$314,200	$356,600	$405,000	$432,700	37.7
5. Honolulu, HI	$295,000	$299,900	$335,000	$392,500	33.0
6. Nassau/Suffolk, NY	$214,000	$248,400	$312,900	$374,400	75.0
7. New York/Northern NJ	$230,200	$258,200	$309,800	$367,400	59.6
8. Los Angeles, CA	$215,900	$241,400	$286,000	$365,300	69.2
9. Bergen/Passaic, NJ	$261,200	$288,800	$337,900	$363,000	38.9
10. Newark, NJ	$242,400	$263,100	$300,500	$355,400	46.6

*Estimate by authors.

Source: National Association of Realtors, www.realtor.org.

Table 2-15   The 10 Least Expensive Metro Areas—Existing Homes

Area	Median Sales Price				
	2000	2001	2002	2003*	2000–2003
1. Buffalo/Niagara Falls, NY	$ 79,800	$ 84,100	$ 85,000	$ 90,600	13.5%
2. Beaumont/Port Arthur, TX	$ 80,800	$ 84,000	$ 84,300	$ 93,400	15.6
3. Springfield, IL	$ 85,000	$ 87,300	$ 90,600	$ 94,300	10.9
4. South Bend, IN	$ 82,200	$ 92,800	$ 91,000	$ 95,700	16.4
5. Ft. Wayne, IN	$ 91,600	$ 93,900	$ 94,900	$ 96,800	5.7
6. Amarillo, TX	$ 86,300	$ 90,200	$ 91,900	$ 97,200	12.6
7. Peoria, IL	$ 87,200	$ 88,600	$ 88,000	$ 97,400	11.7
8. Waterloo/Cedar Falls, IA	$ 80,200	$ 84,500	$ 87,800	$ 98,300	22.6
9. Topeka, KS	$ 80,600	$ 88,700	$ 89,000	$102,100	26.7
10. Shreveport, LA	$ 83,800	$ 88,000	$ 90,300	$102,900	22.8

*Estimate by author.

Source: National Association of Realtors, www.realtor.org.

There are still some places to live where your home won't cost you an arm and a leg. (See Table 2-15.) In 2003, the least expensive metropolitan area was the Buffalo/Niagara Falls, New York, area, where the median price was $90,600, up 13.5 percent from 2000. The second cheapest was Beaumont, Texas, with a median price of $93,400 in 2003. And the gains through appreciation are still decent in some of these areas. In Topeka, Kansas, the median home price rose nearly 27 percent between 2000 and 2003, but still was only $102,100.

If you live in a city where prices aren't going up so fast, you don't have to make a large gain in order to get ahead. If you live in a high-cost area, making the right investment can be vital to getting ahead. The problem comes if you have to move from a low-cost housing area to a high-cost area.

The bottom line is this: If you want a lot of house for less money, and you like snow, move to Buffalo, New York.

CHAPTER 3

Home-Buying Strategies, or 50 Ways to Leave Your Landlord or Your Old House

You've made the decision to buy your first house or to move up to a better existing home or new home. But what path should you take? Here are some snapshot ideas for ways to reach your goal.

1. *Save, save, save.* The first thing you need to do is to put away some cash for your down payment. This may seem simple, but it can be difficult if you don't have a specific plan. On average, Americans save just 3 to 4 percent of their incomes. "A good rule of thumb is to save 10 percent of your income no matter what you make," said Steve Wetzel, a financial planner in Yardley, Pennsylvania.

You must save and save regularly. Here are some examples:
- Set up an interest-paying home-buying bank account or certificate of deposit. Earmark a certain percentage of each paycheck for the fund. You'll be surprised at how fast it adds up.

- If you are married, try to live on one spouse's income and put the other's check into the bank.
- If you rent, pay yourself a higher rent. Say you are paying $1200 a month rent, and the monthly payment on the house you want to buy is $1800 a month. Pay the $1800 now, but put the extra $600 into a savings account.

2. ***Be a bankable buyer.*** Before you can buy a home, you have to get your financial house in order. Make sure you don't have so many debts that the bank won't qualify you for a mortgage. Generally, lenders require that monthly payments on your debts, including credit card charges, total no more than 36 percent of your monthly income. Draw up a monthly budget, and stick to it. If you have more than enough for a down payment, use some of the money to clean up your debts. Pay off your car. Burn all your credit cards, if you have to. Not only will this help you get your mortgage, but it also will create habits that will carry over once you have bought and have to come up with those mortgage payments.

3. ***Get preapproval for a mortgage.*** When it is time to go house shopping, find a lender with competitive rates and get it to preapprove you for a mortgage. This will serve two purposes. First, you will know how big a mortgage the lender will allow, and thus how much you can pay for a house. Second, it will make you a desirable buyer when you are shopping. The seller will know that you can get a loan and may be more inclined to sell to you, even if you offer less than the full asking price. Remember, preapproval isn't the same as prequalifying, which is only an indication of what mortgage you can get.

4. ***Check your equity.*** If you already own a home, calculate how much money you will be able to take out of it. In this case, the equity is the difference between your remaining mortgage and the price you can get for your house. In most cases, your home is automatically "saving" money for you by appreciating in value. This can make a big difference. For example, suppose you bought your house in 1995 for $100,000 with a 10 percent down payment, and you can now sell it for $150,000. Your equity is more than $60,000—your $10,000 down payment plus the $50,000 appreciation plus what you have paid toward principal on the mortgage.

5. *Trading up is still the name of the game.* Most people don't buy their dream house, or anything close to it, the first time they buy a home. Think of the house you are buying today as a step toward a better home. That's why you need to think of your home as an investment. When you are shopping, look at a house the way a future buyer would. You are counting on the appreciation to help you trade up to the next house you want.

Trading up is simply selling your old house, taking the equity (the money you have in the house, including your profit), and buying yourself another, more expensive home.

Consider that house you bought in 1995 for $100,000 and can sell for $150,000. After deducting the expenses of the sale and paying off your old mortgage, you end up with $50,000, which is enough to put down on a house costing $250,000 or more. Then you can start the cycle all over for another move up.

6. *Start small.* Many young people look at the large, comfortable house that their parents own and lament that they could never afford a house like that. Well, their parents couldn't either when they started. The millions of GIs returning home from World War II stood in line for a chance to buy a tiny Levitt subdivision home—three bedrooms and one bath—for $8500, take it or leave it. As their income rose, they moved up and bought bigger houses in which to raise their baby-boom children. That is what you can do. Get into a house, any house, and start building your equity rather than making payments to a landlord.

7. *Buy an older house to start with.* Typically, an existing home is about 20 percent cheaper than a new home, though that varies by area. There are also 50 times as many existing homes as there are new homes on the market in any given year. So the competition gives you more choices and a wide variety of prices. A home that is, say, 25 to 50 years old is often less expensive because it may not have an updated kitchen, multiple bathrooms, and extra rooms. Don't worry; you can add what you need as you build equity.

8. *Buy a house that needs work.* Sometimes the best buy is the house that other people run from. Just because the house is a mess, the walls are chipped, and the carpeting looks a hundred years old may not mean much. The house may be a jewel: good structure, good character, and good design. Focus on what the house could be, not on what it is today. If the house is in a neighborhood where values are likely to rise, the ugly duckling could become a profitable swan.

By today's standards, for example, many old houses have obsolete kitchens. Even a simple new paint job may improve the appearance greatly. At low cost, you can dramatically improve the kitchen by installing new lighting fixtures, new flooring, and new countertops. The same thing applies to old bathrooms. Get rid of all carpeting and you may uncover beautiful hardwood floors.

Be sure to have such a house inspected before you buy it. But you may be able to buy at a low price and sell at a big gain even after making improvements. Just remember that not all improvements you make to a home add to its value.

For instance, according to *Remodeling Contractor* magazine, the return on your investment varies from 126 percent for adding a fireplace and 120 percent for adding a full bath to only 31 percent for adding a swimming pool. A major kitchen remodeling may cost you more than $30,000 but has a 90 percent average payback.

9. *Buy an old house and fix it up*. That's what the coauthor of this book, Ron Shafer, and his wife, Mary Rogers, did. In 2001, they bought a 160-year-old house on historic Route 6A in

Yarmouthport, Massachusetts, on Cape Cod. Since the four-bedroom house was in need of repair, they got it for $240,000, or about $60,000 less than comparable-size "antique" houses in the area.

Two sides of the house were in dire need of new shingles. The interior walls needed repair and painting, the oil furnace was 50 years old, and the driveway was a patch of dirt. But the house had good "bones." It was built in 1840 by Winston Thacher, a relative of a founder of the town. Winston Thacher's family lived in the house, which also was used to make carriage wheels. The house had remained in the Thacher family until 1997. The buyers had begun updates. Most important, they had torn down a wall in the kitchen and cut out the ceiling to create a huge kitchen with the original beams exposed.

In additional to professional help, Ron and Mary paid their college-age son Dan Rogers and his friend Amber Roth to do the shingling. Their teen daughter Kaitlin Rogers helped Ron put up a picket fence. The family added a small deck, a screened porch, a third bathroom, and a stone driveway and converted to gas. Soon the house became a warm, inviting place for visitors such as grown daughter Katie Shafer Rivers. In 2004, the house sold for more than $400,000 (see Figure 3-1).

10. Buy an "affordable" new house. In many areas of the country, local governments require builders to mix in a few homes that are priced lower than the others in a new subdivision. The homes are smaller, and they are generally on smaller lots, but the styles are similar to those of surrounding homes. So don't drive by those high-priced new-home developments too quickly. You just might find an affordable investment in a high-priced subdivision.

11. Buy a finished but unsold new house. Sometimes builders have a cancellation or get ahead of themselves by building too many houses on speculation. In such a case, you may be able to negotiate a discount price because it is very costly for builders

Figure 3-1 Yarmouthport, MA, circa 1840

to carry unsold units—they have to pay interest on the money they borrowed to build the house. Or they may have to turn the unsold units over to the lender, who then must get rid of them.

12. Find a home in a turnaround neighborhood. The key to good investing is to buy low and sell high. One way to get a good buy is to purchase a home in an area that has been on a downswing but is starting back.

In 2003, James B. Flynn and Kevin Wynne bought a 102-year-old house near downtown Columbus, Ohio, in a neighborhood that had once been known as "the silk stocking residential district" because so many prominent citizens lived there. But over the years, the neighborhood had declined, with many of the old homes being chopped up into rooming houses and apartments. Now the area is undergoing a renaissance.

Jim and Kevin had previously owned a 1600-square-foot home in a gentrified area of the city. They considered buying a new 2000-square-foot home in the same neighborhood, but the price was $350,000. Instead, they bought a 4000-square-foot three-story jewel in the reviving neighborhood for $168,000 (see Figure 3-2).

The three-story house has six bedrooms, a three-car garage, and many original features, "right down to every original door knob," Jim said. The house is a "Georgian, brick, American foursquare built in 1898. It is very Edwardian, almost art nouveau or Belle Epoch. The house had been built for a local family, the Wallicks, who had owned a large hotel called the Deschler Wallick."

Since Jim and Kevin had sold their old house at a profit, they had some money that they could use to refurbish the new place,

Figure 3-2 Kevin's and Jim's house in Columbus, Ohio

along with putting in hours of work themselves. They also got help from the family. Jim's mother, Leona Flynn of Troy, New York, and Kevin's mom, Sharon Rummery of Pataskala, Ohio, pitched in to help with the painting and cleaning.

Jim and Kevin clearly are enjoying their home buy. As Kevin remarked: "We even got another great benefit: much lower taxes and, oh, well, maybe next year we'll put in a marble bath on the third floor."

Predicting whether a neighborhood will come back is tricky. Experts whose business it is to spot and invest in growth areas offer these guidelines.

Most restorations don't occur in the worst slum areas. Instead, the rehabilitation is usually in working-class neighborhoods just beyond the central city.

It is best to get in early, but there is no sure-fire formula for determining that a neighborhood will revive. If you go into an area that has been depressed, there is often a section that has been restored. Driving five or ten blocks in a circle will show you the potential growth areas. Once the comeback begins, you will probably see growth in that area. Just be certain that you have the home inspected to make sure it is fundamentally sound.

13. *Buy a future.* What a house and its neighborhood are like today is important. But what they will look like tomorrow is equally important. Will the area—and its housing values—keep growing, or is it peaking or even declining? Think ahead to changes that will improve a neighborhood—a new subway or a bus line, a new shopping center, better commuting roads, or nearby construction of more expensive houses that will pull up the value of your home—and buy before the changes come and increase property values. Look at what a house can become and what you can do with it. Can you remodel the kitchen? Could you easily enclose the porch? Could you add another room? Are the bathrooms expandable? Smart buyers develop an eye for such things and can see the potential value in a house and an area. Be aware of the possibilities and dream a little.

14. Avoid gimmicks and extremes. Some houses are fixed up to sell you on glitzy gimmicks rather than on substance. The seller hopes that you will be so dazzled by the gimmicks that you won't notice the drabness or the defects. There are several strategic places where these "fixers" try to distract your attention:

- *The front door.* You see the fancy front door, and it looks great. It may have cost $800, but it's worth it to the seller if it impresses you when you walk into the house. The fancy entry may be a doorway to disaster. Just remember, you are buying much more than a front door.
- *Wall coverings.* Beautiful wallpaper may look very expensive, but it may cover things you should be looking for.
- *Outside lights.* They look pretty, especially in the evening, but they probably are just good-looking lighting fixtures that you can pick up at Home Depot.
- A *fancy chandelier.* Oh, what a beauty! This you also can get in a nearby store for less than $500. Remember that.
- *The kitchen.* Here is the place where the "fixers" really get to promote their handiwork. Don't be misled by what you see. Look for quality. It's not hard to "remodel" a kitchen by putting up a couple of new cabinets, slapping down some floor tiles, and installing a new stove. But this "remodeling" may add $50,000 to the price.

The point is not to let one head-turning feature distract you from taking a close, hard look at a house. Buy substance, not style. And when you go to sell the house in the future, remember that most buyers prefer the traditional to the bizarre.

15. Get in early. Prices in the first part of a new housing subdivision are often lower. The builder is testing the market. He wants to get off to a good sales start in order to show that this will be an accepted community. So get there early. The homes in the first section will probably be a better deal.

16. *Do your homework.* Find out what houses in the neighborhood in which you want to buy are selling for. These days, it's easy to find home sale prices on the Internet. But you need more than the asking price; you need to find out what the houses really sold for, which is often below the asking price. You can often find these data on the Internet, too. Many local newspapers list home sales and the prices, or you can check with a real estate agent.

Visit open houses and compare houses and prices. Then when a house you like comes on the market, you will be able to recognize that it is a good buy, or you will know that the house is overpriced and open to negotiation for a lower price. Eventually, you will become expert enough to spot the good buys.

17. *Buy farther out—it's usually cheaper.* In most areas, the farther you go from town, the cheaper the houses are because land is cheaper in the more distant areas, and there is less demand. The result is that you can sometimes buy a big house that would cost you up to twice as much in a neighborhood closer to town. In the high-priced Washington, D.C., area of Alexandria, Virginia, for example, a typical four-bedroom house with two-and-a-half baths and a two-car garage would cost over $400,000, while miles away in Stafford, Virginia, a similar house would go for under $250,000. If you buy in an area where demand is picking up, then you can gain enough on your cheaper house to allow you to move in closer if you want to.

18. *Buy off season.* The best housing sales market is in the spring. And that is when the prices are strongest. During the summer doldrums or the dead of winter, houses are hard to sell.

If you can wait until the slow period—cold days in November, December, and January or dog days in August when everybody else is at the beach—you may get a better deal. Demand is lower, and sellers are willing to negotiate a lower price. Go house shopping during or after a period of heavy snow, when nobody is buying and the demoralized sellers are spending weekends sitting in open houses.

19. ***Buy directly from the owner.*** Our real estate friends will be annoyed, but sometimes the way to get a lower price is to buy from an owner-seller. You can save at least part or even all of the cost of the agent's commission, which is usually 6 percent of the selling price. So if you buy a home for $150,000, your potential saving is as much as $9000. The problem with FSBO (for sale by owner) houses is that the owners sometimes not only don't want to cut their price, but also have overpriced the house in the first place. So approach FSBOs cautiously.

20. ***Buy with unit pricing.*** One way to figure what is the best buy for the money is to shop for houses the way you shop for groceries—use unit pricing to compare products. To do this for a house, you need to know at least two things: the price and the total living area in square feet. (You may add to this the square feet of the lot.) If, for example, the price is $210,000 (this is the median price of new homes) and the living area totals 1800 square feet, the unit cost per square foot is $116.67. (Divide $210,000 by 1800.) Then you can compare the cost per square foot of several homes to help you determine which is the most house for the money.

21. ***Assume a mortgage.*** One way to get a low-interest mortgage loan is to take over somebody else's mortgage. If rates go up to, say, 8 percent, and somebody is selling a home she bought in the early 2000s with an assumable mortgage of 5 percent or even lower, you can save hundreds of dollars a month by taking over the mortgage. You also save on closing costs.

There are some potential pitfalls. You may have to come up with a big down payment if there is a big gap between the amount of the remaining mortgage and the sale price of the house. In addition, some loans have a "due on sale clause," which means that the lender may not let the mortgage be assumed. But most adjustable-rate mortgages are assumable. The best bets are fixed-rate FHA and VA loans, which are assumable.

22. *Buy during bad times.* It may sound crazy, but the best time to buy is when the housing market is in a slump. Sharp buyers stay out of the market when everybody is in and then jump in when everybody is avoiding it.

When there are plenty of buyers, housing sells quickly at top prices. But when housing sales are slow, sellers are desperate— this can be the *best* time to buy. Prices level off, and sellers are willing to bargain. This is also a good time to shop the new-housing market. If sales are down, builders may be willing to cut their selling price to avoid the higher costs they must pay to carry completed but unsold houses.

Remember, a housing slump can be the worst time for sellers, but the best time for buyers, especially first-time buyers who don't have to sell their existing home in a down market.

23. *Make a wildly low offer.* This applies particularly during bad times, but it can work anytime. Find a house that has been on the market for a long time or one that is priced far above the others in an area. Then make an offer that is way below the asking price. You may not get your price, but you may get a counteroffer that is surprisingly close to it. In any case, you probably will be able to buy a home at less than the asking price.

In 1998, a couple went shopping for a house in McLean, Virginia, and fell in love with a New England colonial that was over their budget at $740,000. After checking at the county courthouse, they discovered that the sellers had bought the house for $800,000 a decade earlier, before the local housing market took a dive, and had been trying to sell the house for over 2 years. So they decided to submit an offer on the house at $100,000 under the asking price.

The offer was accepted. They bought the house for $640,000. In 2001, after the housing market heated up, the couple sold the house for $840,000.

24. Make an offer they can't refuse. In a hot housing market, houses sometimes sell for *more than* the asking price. Sometimes the best strategy to get the house you really want is to quickly offer the full price and even offer to pay some of the seller's closing costs. If the house is in a growing area, this may be a small price to pay. After all, the total price is usually amortized over 30 years, and you probably won't be there that long. And you will probably get your money back many times over as the price goes up in value.

25. Lease to buy. If you don't have much cash for a down payment, one option may be a lease-purchase arrangement. The lease-to-buy agreement will generally specify the price you will pay, say, 1 to 3 years later. It will also give you a chance to see whether you really like the place or not.

When you lease with an option to buy, you pay an option fee for the right to buy the house at a specified time for an agreed-upon price. You can have part of your rent go toward the down payment, though if you do, you will have to pay a higher rent.

This arrangement gives you time to save for the down payment and also locks in a price, which protects you if housing prices should go up. If you decide against buying, you lose your option fee and the cost of the rent.

26. Go condo. One of the cheapest ways (in most places) to get started in home buying is with a condominium or small town house. Luxury condos can cost a bundle, but condos at the starter level are about the only homes you can buy for under $100,000 in some areas. Also, in a switch from the past, condos have become good investments that appreciate in price.

27. Buy a duplex and rent out one side. A duplex is a double house with a living unit on each side. You can rent out one side to help you pay for the whole place. Also look for a town house with a twist: You can live in the upper levels and rent out the lower level. These kinds of town houses usually have an entry on the side or the back. But you have to have your own address, and your renter does, too.

As an owner/occupant you can qualify for a mortgage using the easier homeowner qualifications with as low as 5 percent down. You will receive rent income from your tenant. This income will be counted as part of your regular income on your mortgage application, which will allow you to qualify for a larger mortgage. The rent will also help you to pay your mortgage. As an owner/occupant, you can use your homeowner's insurance to insure your duplex while you live in it. A duplex is an excellent tax shelter, as it shows a paper loss when you calculate your depreciation.

28. Start rolling with a mobile home. The cheapest way to get started in home buying is with a mobile home. These are not your father's old house trailers. They're now called "manufactured homes," and they come in all sizes and styles. While they may have wheels, most of them are never moved once they are delivered. And forget about those seedy old trailer parks. Today's mobile home parks are like housing subdivisions, with lush lawns, sidewalks, and paved streets.

The median cost of a manufactured home is about $53,000, less than a third of the median price of an existing house, according to the Bureau of the Census. You also have to pay a fee to park the home; the median fee in manufactured-home communities is about $280 a month.

29. Buy a foreclosed home. You may get a good buy on a house that somebody else couldn't afford to keep. When lenders aren't paid, they take over the house and then try to sell it. The federal agencies and others that insure mortgages or buy them also sell many foreclosed houses. But you have to know what you are buying. In some cases, the foreclosed house may be in bad shape. Or it may be in a less desirable area.

One place to find out about these houses is at the federal Department of Housing and Urban Development web site (www.hud.gov). To buy a HUD home, you must contact a real estate broker in your area who is authorized to sell HUD homes (most are). Your broker will submit the bid for you. The HUD web site will also lead you to homes sold by other government agencies.

Another place to check is Freddie Mac, the government-sponsored but private mortgage financing company. It offers homes for sale on a web site called www.homesteps.com. You can find foreclosed homes on lenders' web sites, too.

Some lenders and government agencies will let you buy a foreclosed home with no down payment if your credit is good and they're anxious to have the home occupied.

30. Bid for a house that's on the auction block. When a builder goes bankrupt, the homes are sometimes auctioned to the highest bidder. Frequently, the highest bid may be a lower price than you could have bought the house for originally.

A new twist has been added to auctions in the past few years: online auctions. "At online auctioneer sites you'll find property listings with floor plans, photos, and sometimes even a virtual tour," states the web site www.thisoldhouse.com. "If you're ready to take the plunge from real-life auctions to their online counterparts, there are a few important things you should know. First, online auctions include pre-registration followed by bidding for a specified period of time, but the 'winning' bid isn't a final transaction. The sale isn't binding until a contract is signed."

Other places to check on the Internet include IbidCo (www.ibidco.com), which specializes in new communities under construction by major developers; Rbuy (www.rbuy.com), which shows listings of new homes, resales, investment properties, luxury properties, and foreclosures; RealtyBid International (www.RealtyBid.com), which specializes in the online sale of institutionally owned real estate; and Bid4assets (www.bid4assets.com).

31. Get the longest mortgage you can. If you want to hold down the monthly payment, you want to stretch the payments over the longest period possible. This is usually 30 years. The length of the mortgage may be the deciding factor in getting the most expensive house you can afford. For example, on a 20-year loan for $80,000 with a 6 percent interest rate, the monthly payment for principal and interest is $758. With a 30-year loan at 6 percent, the monthly payment is $664, a difference of $94 a month. Sure, you will pay more interest over the life of the mortgage, but chances are you won't have the mortgage that long anyway. Besides, the interest is tax-deductible.

32. *Get the shortest mortgage you can.* If you want to build equity quickly or if you plan to stay in the house you buy for a long time, the shortest-term loan may be best for you. With a 15-year mortgage, you have a higher monthly payment than with a 30-year loan, but your equity grows much faster. You also get a lower interest rate. You can use the equity to trade up to a bigger house. Or you can save thousands of dollars in interest costs and own your house free and clear in 15 years.

33. *Get an interest-only mortgage.* If you expect to resell your house in 5 to 10 years, one way to save on monthly mortgage payments is get a loan on which you pay only the monthly interest. You save the cost of monthly payments toward principal, and all of your loan payment is tax-deductible. This also means that you are not paying down the mortgage, so eventually you will want to either sell your house or switch to a regular mortgage with higher payments.

34. *Make a big down payment.* If you're worried about making those monthly mortgage payments, one way to hold down the monthly outflow is to make the biggest down payment you can. A big down payment may also make the difference in qualifying for a loan.

For example, on a $100,000 house, a 10 percent down payment leaves you with a $90,000 mortgage. With a 30-year mortgage at 7 percent interest, the payments, including property taxes and insurance, would be about $790 a month. You would need a household income of at least $33,852 to qualify. But if you put down 20 percent, or $20,000, the payment on your mortgage would be about $684 a month. You could qualify with an income of about $29,328. At 25 percent down, your monthly housing expenses would be $651, and you would need an income of $27,900.

35. *Make a small down payment.* The main advantage of a small down payment is obvious: You have to come up with less dough in order to buy a house. On a $100,000 house, you need $20,000 for a 20 percent down payment, but only $10,000 for a 10 percent down payment. In fact, if you had to come up with a 20 percent down payment, perhaps you couldn't even buy the $100,000 house. So sometimes you can get into a bigger and better house by putting less down. Just be sure you can afford the bigger mortgage payment.

There are other reasons to opt for a low down payment. You also get *leverage*, which in real estate means using the least investment to make the most money. For instance, if after a couple of years the $100,000 house goes up in value by 10 percent, or $10,000, the return on a $20,000 down payment is 50 percent. With $10,000 down, the return is 100 percent.

Other reasons you might want to make a low down payment and conserve your cash include the following:

- You will need at least 5 percent of the loan amount for all kinds of expenses, such as appraisal fees and settlement charges.
- You will need even more money to move. You may have to buy new furniture, drapes, and other things. And they all cost money.
- You don't want to tie up all your cash in your house. You may need some for emergencies and other investments.

36. *Get a no-down-payment VA loan.* An estimated 30 million military veterans are eligible for Veterans Administration, or VA, mortgages. If you are one of them, you can get a loan with a low down payment or no down payment at all. The mortgage rate is usually a bit below the market rate, so you can save on the monthly payments. Lenders like VA loans because there is little red tape and they are guaranteed by the agency.

Even if you have already used your loan benefits, it may be possible for you to buy a home again with VA financing by using your remaining or restored loan entitlement. No VA loan can exceed $240,000.

37. Get an FHA loan. If you're not a veteran, you can still get mortgage help from Uncle Sam. The Federal Housing Administration of the Department of Housing and Urban Development insures home loans. Since the FHA is providing insurance, you can get a loan with as little as 3 percent down. There are several programs that offer buyers no down payment at all. The maximum FHA loan limit varies depending on the county in which you are purchasing. The current FHA loan limit for a single-family home, condo, or town house can be as much as $239,250.

The main advantage of an FHA home loan is that the credit criteria for a borrower are not as strict as those for conventional loans. Someone who has had a few credit problems should not have a problem obtaining FHA financing. In addition, the seller must pay for part of the traditional closing costs.

38. Get private mortgage insurance. If you don't have much cash but you can afford the payments, you can pay as little as 10 or even 5 percent down with the help of private mortgage insurance. Without it, most lenders require a down payment of 20 to 25 percent of the purchase price of the house. Basically, the private mortgage insurance company insures the difference (for a fee, of course). This insurance may help you get into a house. You pay the fee as part of your monthly mortgage payment.

Private mortgage insurance remains a part of your mortgage payment until the equity in your home reaches at least 20 percent. In many cases, when that happens, you must write to the servicing lender and request that the PMI premium be removed.

You can find out more about private mortgage insurance on the web site www.privatemi.com.

39. *Take a piggyback ride.* One way to avoid mortgage insurance and still make a low down payment is to get two "piggy-backed" loans. With these loans (also known as 80-10-10 loans), you put down 10 percent of the home's price. Next, you take out a 30-year loan for 80 percent of the home price. Finally, you get a 15-year fixed-rate loan at a higher interest rate. The two loans together make up your monthly payment. As a result, the mortgage payment is usually higher than with a traditional loan, but the total is less than if you had to buy private mortgage insurance.

40. *A call to ARMs.* You can usually get a lower interest rate if you buy your house with an adjustable-rate mortgage (ARM). Unlike the traditional fixed-rate mortgage, with an ARM the rate can go up or down after an initial period. Lenders talk of a 3-and-1 ARM or a 5-and-1 ARM. This means that the initial rate stays the same for 3 years or 5 years, then it is adjusted based on an agreed-upon index. The loan should have "caps" limiting how much the rate can go up in a year and how much it can go up in total. Be sure to figure whether you could afford the loan if the interest rate were to go up to the peak. ARMs are an especially good option if you don't expect to be in your house for a long time.

41. *Get help with the down payment.* There are several programs available for buyers who don't have the required down payment for a house. One is the Nehemiah Corporation down payment assistance program, which provides qualifying home buyers with free funds for use toward the down payment and closing costs for eligible loan programs. AmeriDream Charity Inc., a nonprofit corporation, provides down payment assistance to low- and moderate-income home buyers who demonstrate the need for financial assistance. Housing Action Resource Trust (HART), a nonprofit corporation, promotes home ownership through its down payment assistance program for low- and moderate-income home buyers. You can find out more about such help by checking www.hud.gov.

Fannie Mae, the giant government-sponsored private corporation that buys mortgages, offers "expanded approval" and "flex 100" programs that cover mortgages up to 100 percent of the value of the home. Home buyers must come up with about 3 percent of the total in cash for closing costs, but that can come from a grant.

GMAC Mortgage Corp. offers Home-Stretch loans. The buyer gets an FHA-insured mortgage to cover about 98 percent of the purchase price. GMAC then adds a second mortgage to cover the down payment and closing costs. The second mortgage is forgiven starting in the sixth year if the family has kept up its payments.

More help may be on the way thanks to an American Dream Down Payment Initiative that President George W. Bush signed into law in late 2003. The measure authorizes $200 million in grants to state and local agencies to help home buyers with their down payment and closing costs. The average subsidy is expected to be about $7500.

42. Get help from Fannie Mae. You can try to get help with the down payment from your church, your synagogue, or some other nonprofit organization. If you do, Fannie Mae has what it calls a 3/2 loan program. This program allows you to make a down payment of only 3 percent if another nonprofit organization will put down the other 2 percent of the required down payment.

43. Ask your parents for help. When you're ready to move out of the nest to your own nest, mom and dad often can help you. Funds obtained as a gift from any relative, or from anyone with whom you have "an established personal relationship," are acceptable to lenders as part of your down payment or closing costs. However, you will generally have to make a down payment of at least 5 percent of the sales price unless the gift alone amounts to 20 percent of the sales price. Or your parents could co-sign the loan with you.

44. *Get money from your Uncle IRA.* You can withdraw money from your individual retirement account (IRA). If you are a first-time home buyer, you can take out $10,000 of these funds penalty-free under certain conditions. If you are not a first-time home buyer, you should take out as little as you need for a down payment.

45. *Get a second mortgage.* One way to borrow money for a down payment is by taking out a second mortgage. Usually, these are small mortgages that are repayable in 2 to 10 years. Rates generally run a couple of percentage points higher than your mortgage rate. Sometimes you can get the seller of the house to take back a second mortgage as part of the down payment.

46. *Teachers and cops on the block.* In many areas of the country, teachers and police officers can't afford to buy houses in the communities in which they work. Under a federal program, full-time teachers, school administrators, and police officers can buy homes owned by HUD in "revitalized" neighborhoods for 50 percent of the sales price. They can also obtain special mortgages. The buyers must agree to live in the home for at least 3 years. Teachers must also work in the area in which the home is located.

More than 6000 police officers and teachers in 41 states and the District of Columbia have purchased homes under these two programs since they were created in 1997 and 2000. More details can be found at www.hud.gov.

47. *Get a break from a builder.* Because builders arrange lines of credit in volume, they can often offer a discount mortgage rate. Sometimes, to move houses, builders also offer a "buy-down." A buy-down is a subsidy of the mortgage interest rate that helps you meet the payments during the first few years of the loan. For example, if the prevailing rate is 8 percent, the builder may offer to subsidize the rate down to 6 percent for the first 2 or 3 years, saving you a sizable amount of your mortgage payment. Just make sure that you can afford the higher payment when it begins. Make sure the subsidy is part of the contract with your lender as well as with your builder. And make sure that the subsidy isn't offset by a price that is higher than that for a comparable house elsewhere.

48. *Buy with sweat equity.* The ultimate sweat equity is to build your house yourself, and some people do. But usually "sweat equity" means only that you have to do some of the work in return for a price break or access to a home purchase.

Under sweat equity programs, your labor may be counted as the down payment or used to help pay other costs. Most current programs now involve a nonprofit community development organization and always require the cooperation of a lender.

Mike's Favorite Sweat Equity Story

Back in Ohio in the late 1950s, the builder I worked for had a program that let buyers get a house with a lower down payment if they would perform certain tasks, such as painting, landscaping, and cleaning. One Monday, when I returned to the job, I noticed that one house had been painted an ugly reddish color. An angry couple was waiting for me at the superintendent shack.

"Who painted our house such an ugly color?"

"We sure didn't," I said.

As it happened, the potential owner of a nearby unit had painted the wrong house.

The best-known sweat equity program is Habitat for Humanity International, which is promoted by former President Jimmy Carter. It offers lower-income families a way to pay part of the cost of the home by helping volunteers and professionals to build the house they will live in or other houses that the agency is building. For information, see www.habitat.org.

49. *Snare a subsidy.* Many states and counties have housing-subsidy programs aimed especially at first-time buyers or lower-income buyers (those with a mean income that can be as much as $40,000 a year or more in some areas). In most state or local programs that offer below-market mortgage interest rates, the program buys houses and then sells them to moderate-income buyers. You can find available programs in your state by checking the federal Department of Housing and Urban Development web site (www.hud.gov) or the National Association of State Housing Agencies (www.ncsha.org).

50. *Trade down.* It used to be that trading down to a cheaper house would cost you money because if your old house had gone up in value, you would have to pay a capital gains tax on the net profit from its sale. To put off the tax bite, you had to buy a house that cost as much as or more than the one you sold. That changed in the 1990s when Congress eliminated taxes on home profits of up to $500,000 for couples and $250,000 for individuals, if you have lived in the house for at least 2 years. Now when the kids have flown the nest, a couple can keep much of the profit and move down to a smaller home with a cheaper mortgage. Or if you are a homeowner in a high-cost area, you can move to a cheaper but equal-sized house—or a bigger one—in a low-cost area and have money left over.

Nobody can decide which house is best for you. Only you can decide that. Salespeople can't tell you. We can't tell you. Ignore our advice if you want to. Buy a home that you want to live in—something that you will feel comfortable with and something that suits your lifestyle. Don't get a big yard if you hate yard work. Don't buy a handyman's special if you have two left hands.

Buy a house that you will feel at home in. After all, it's your house—or it will be soon.

CHAPTER 4

Mouse Hunt, House Hunt

Shopping on the Internet

When we first wrote *The Complete Book of Home Buying* in 1979, the Internet was just a gleam in Al Gore's eye. Now it is an indispensable tool for house hunting. Just plug in "home buying," and the hits keep on coming.

With just a few clicks of your mouse, you can find just about everything you need to know about home buying and mortgages. You can find details about houses for sale, complete with photos. You can investigate living areas right down to local neighborhoods, including the quality of education, crime, the cost of living, health and safety, the economy, and transportation. And you can do all this right from a chair in your home or at the library.

Naturally, you'll eventually have to look at prospective homes up close and personal. But as coauthor Mike Sumichrast discovered, the Internet has revolutionized today's house-hunting world.

All of the major power engines—MSN, AOL, Netscape, Yahoo, and others—can lead you to real estate data sites. MSN's "House and Home" is especially useful. These sites include calculators that let you figure what you can afford, what your payments would be at different prices and interest rates, and just

Mike's Favorite Surfing Story

Columbus, Ohio, is about as middle class as you can find anywhere in the United States. A detailed search of the National Realtors Association's www.Realtor.com web site shows that some homes that sold for around $12,500 to $14,000 when I was involved in construction in Columbus in the mid-1950s are now selling for about $160,000. Our subdivision was on the outskirts of the city. I wondered at that time who would drive that far from the center of the city.

This area has grown quite a bit since then and now has 22,768 people with 2.37 persons per household. I discovered that the median household income is $41,279. Only 47.57 percent of the people living there are married. The school achievement index is low, yet the cost per student is higher than the national average. The median home purchase cost is $86,006. This area is described as Blue-Chip Blues, with mostly Upscale Blue-Collar Families. Until I looked at this detailed information for various localities, I didn't know that where I live in Potomac, Maryland, is classified as Elite Super-Rich Families. I don't think I am one of them.

about anything else you want to know. You can even apply for a mortgage online.

House-Hunting Sites

FREDDIE MAC

One of the best web sites is www.freddiemac.com, run by the government-sponsored private corporation that buys home mortgages from lenders. Click on "Buying and Owning a Home" under "Resources for Homeownership," and you'll find a link to "Your Route to Homeownership."

Through this site, you can research basic home-buying information, such as what you can afford. You can learn about credit requirements and find out about mortgages. The site offers other data as well, including current mortgage rates.

Freddie has a useful sister, too, called www.homesteps.com. One feature is something called "Home Detective." You plug in "clues" to the kind of home you are looking for in a certain area, and you will receive free emails when homes matching your clues become available.

FANNIE MAE

This is another government-sponsored private mortgage giant that provides tons of home-buying data on its web site, www.homepath.com. This ranges from a "home visit work sheet" to help in finding Fannie Mae–approved lenders. One especially useful tool is the Fannie Mae True Cost Calculator, which helps you figure the true cost of a mortgage loan. With the calculator, you "compare different types of loans in terms of monthly payments, tax implications, closing costs and other fees."

An affiliated Fannie Mae site, www.fanniemaefoundation.org, provides access to several colorful and easy-to-understand guides on home buying and financing, such as "Opening the Door to a Home of Your Own." The guides come in nine languages: English, Spanish, Chinese, Korean, Russian, Polish, Vietnamese, Portuguese, and Haitian-Creole.

NATIONAL ASSOCIATION OF REALTORS

The Big Daddy of home-hunting sites is www.Realtor.com, where you can find data on more than two million homes for sale across the country. It used to be that only real estate agents could look up houses on what's called the Multiple Listing Service, or MLS. Now you can save your shoe leather and tour hundreds of homes, complete with photos and MapPoint locations, including much of the MLS. You get details on the sale price, the expected mortgage payment, the interior rooms, the garage, and other features. Often you can take a "virtual tour" of color photos of the inside of the house as well.

You also can find detailed information on neighborhoods, schools, and whether the market in that area is hot or cold. For example, looking for a home in the suburbs of Baltimore, Maryland, in the $200,000 range would bring you to Linthicum Heights, a neighborhood where the average home price is $205,740.46, the median age is 39.4 years, the median household income is nearly $37,600, and most homes are in "older, established" areas.

An affiliated site, www.Homestore.com, features not only the Realtor site but other housing data links as well—for example, data on new homes, manufactured homes, senior housing, and home improvements. Its computer tools range from "Credit Analyzer" and "The Relocation Wizard" to "The School Report" and "Neighborhood Finder."

Government on the Web

HUD

A good place to start a home search is at the U.S. Department of Housing and Urban Development's web site, www.hud.gov. HUD provides lots of basic information for home buyers. Click on "Buying" under "Homes" and find out how much house you can afford, on "Wish list" to find the house you want, on "Home-shopping check list," or on "Homebuyer's rights." You can watch a video about buying a home. You can also obtain information about Federal Housing Administration (FHA) mortgages.

GINNIE MAE

You should also try HUD's sister mortgage agency, Ginnie Mae, at www.ginniemae.gov. It also has "Your Path to Homeownership," which takes you step by step through the home-buying process (see Table 4-1). Its calculators allow you to figure out

Table 4-1   Home Ownership Chart

Home Ownership 101	Finding a Home
• **Choosing the Right Mortgage** • **Who's Involved in the Process** • **Basic Mortgage Math** • **Homebuyer's Reference** • **The Refinance Process** • **Glossary of Terms**	• **Choosing the Right Home for You** • **Choosing a Real Estate Agent** • **The Negotiation Process** • **FAQs by First-Time Homebuyers** • **Additional Homebuyer Information**
Applying for a Loan	*Making the Purchase*
• **Required Paperwork** • **Criteria for Loan Applications** • **Getting Your Loan Approved** • **Reasons a Loan May Not Be Approved** • **Options If Your Loan Is Not Approved**	• **Pre-Closing** • **Closing Participants** • **What Happens at Closing** • **Paperwork You Will Sign** • **Paperwork You Will Sign (Part 2)** • **Post-Closing**

Source: www.ginniemae.gov.

what you can afford with an FHA home loan or a VA loan as well as with a conventional mortgage.

U.S. GENERAL SERVICES ADMINISTRATION

The General Services Administration (GSA) operates the Federal Citizen Information Center in Pueblo, Colorado, which offers all kinds of consumer guides at www.pueblo.gsa.gov. Housing guides range from "100 Questions and Answers about Buying a New Home" to "Homeowner's Glossary of Building Terms."

DEPARTMENT OF VETERAN AFFAIRS

If you're a veteran, you'll want to check out the Department of Veteran Affairs for information on VA mortgages. At www.home-loansva.gov, you can get information on who is eligible for VA loans and how to get these loans, which are made by private lenders.

FEDERAL RESERVE BOARD

A good place to look for information on conventional mortgages is the Federal Reserve Board, the agency that holds power over interest rates. Its home page, www.federalreserve.gov, is a bit daunting, but if you click on "Consumer Information," you can find mortgage help, including a mortgage-shopping worksheet.

FEDERAL TRADE COMMISSION

The FTC is a consumer protection agency that polices all kinds of consumer issues. But you also can find information on how to avoid being scammed on housing. Go to its web site at www.ftc.gov and you'll find reports on such topics as mortgage scams plus reports such as "Auction Guides: Not So Hot Properties" and "Looking for the Best Mortgage."

MORE FEDERAL AGENCIES

There are a couple of government web sites where you can find loads of housing statistics. An excellent source is the U.S. Census

Bureau site, www.census.gov. Another is the White House site at www.whitehouse.gov. Click on "Social Statistics Briefing Room," and you will find all kinds of data, including data on home owner-ship and other housing matters. You can find data on education at the Department of Education, www.ed.gov. As for crime statistics, check out the Federal Bureau of Investigation at www.fbi.gov.

STATE AND LOCAL GOVERNMENTS

These entities are increasingly putting housing information online. Usually, you can find out exactly what the seller paid for the house you are buying and what other people paid for comparable properties. You also can check what different houses are assessed at for tax purposes. State and local governments also have housing programs that provide subsidies and assist with down payments.

Trade Groups

NATIONAL ASSOCIATION OF HOME BUILDERS

The National Association of Home Builders (NAHB) presents most of its consumer information on Homestore Inc.'s www.homebuilder.com. There you can find out how to buy a newly built home and look for builders in your area. You can look at more than 11,000 home plans at the link called (what else?) www.homeplans.com. And, of course, you can get a firsthand photo look at thousands of new homes (see Figure 4-1). At the NAHB's own web site, www.nahb.org, you can find consumer guides on subjects from "Choosing a Builder" to "Mortgage Basics."

MORTGAGE BANKERS ASSOCIATION

The Mortgage Bankers Association (MBA) is another good place to find out about mortgages at www.mbaa.com and www.homeloanlearningcenter.com. You will find such tools as a

Figure 4-1   Dream House

Photo by James F. Wilson.
Source: Builder Magazine.

rent vs. own calculator, explanations of different types of mortgages, and a "Plain & Simple Guide" for first-time home buyers
or all home buyers.

Part of the guide steers buyers through the scary process of
asking a lender for money. We won't repeat the old joke about
the heart-transplant patient who was asked if he wanted the
heart of an astronaut, a star football player, or a 60-year-old
banker. He said the banker, "because his heart has never been
used." Nosiree, we won't repeat that story. Not us.

But as the MBA puts it: "You're going to meet a complete
stranger. You're asking for more money than you've ever seen in
your life. And all your hopes are riding on the answer. No wonder
you're nervous about getting your first mortgage!"

The site provides various planning tools to help home buyers
through the process:

Getting Started
How to Make Your First Meeting Work
Decisions, Decisions, Decisions . . .
First Class Help for First Time Buyers
Applying Yourself
The Low-down on Loans
How to Choose Your Lender
Fifteen Commonly Used Mortgage Terms

Source: Mortgage Bankers Association.

MANUFACTURED HOUSING INSTITUTE

At the manufactured housing industry's web site, www.manufac-turedhousing.org, you can find out all about the housing that until 1976 was known as mobile homes. As the photos show, today it's hard to tell a manufactured home from a regular house. Yet prices range from $15,000 to $100,000. And, according to the site, "In 2000, 22 million Americans (about 8.0 percent of the U.S. population) lived full-time in 10.0 million manufactured homes." The site explains how HUD has beefed up construction rules and provides guides such as "How to Buy a Manufactured Home."

HOME INSPECTORS

There are two major web sites for home inspection groups. At the National Association of Home Inspectors site, www.nahi.org, a guide called "Most Important Visitor" tells you what to expect from a home inspection of a house you plan to buy. At the site for the American Society of Home Inspectors, www.ashi.org, you can even get "Mold Information." A Q&A takes you through the home-inspection process:

Q. Do I need to be there?
A. It is not necessary for you to be present for the inspection, but it is recommended. You will be able to observe the inspector and ask questions directly, as you

learn about the condition of the home, how its systems work, and how to maintain it. You will also find the written report easier to understand if you've seen the property first-hand through the inspector's eyes.

Both groups tell you how to find a certified home inspector in your area.

BETTER BUSINESS BUREAU

Your local Better Business Bureau is a good place to check if you have any questions about a builder, a real estate agency, a mortgage lender, or some other housing service provider. The national BBB's web site at www.bbb.org provides such general housing guides as "Real Estate Agents and Brokers," "Mortgage Choices," and "Home Warranties."

Nothing but Net

Internet housing services are popping up all over the Information Superhighway. These services let you look at databases on neighborhoods, home prices, property taxes, and other data all over the country.

At www.bestplaces.net, compiled by Bert Sperling, you'll find one of the best web sites for comparative data on cities, neighborhoods, schools, and other useful information. From a list of 3000 city profiles you can compare cities on such factors as housing, cost of living, and crime rates. You can get data on 87,000 U.S. public schools in 16,000 school districts. You can compare crime rates in 2500 cities. You can look up "Your Best Place to Live."

At www.Domania.com, you can check more than 27 million U.S. home purchase price records free. The database is continually updated. When you are looking at specific houses, you can check what the real estate industry calls "comps," or comparable houses, to see how the prices compare. You can check not only asking prices but, more important, the actual purchase prices.

At www.GoneHome.com, you can shop thousands of for sale by owner homes, or FSBOs. You can find a buyer's agent, an agent who doesn't represent the seller, to help you find a home. And you can shop for mortgages.

At www.NeighborhoodScout.com, you can plug in the features you are looking for in a neighborhood, and the computer will find neighborhoods where you might want to live. One feature is "How to Find Excellent Public Schools." NeighborhoodScout says that it "rates the quality of every public school district in America and lets you search for communities with the best school districts, anywhere in the country."

At www.bankrate.com, you can compare mortgage rates across the country, but this informative web site also provides much more. There are tips on home shopping, such as "6 Keys to Happy Home Buying." There is advice, such as "A timeline for buying a new home," "10 questions sellers hope you don't ask," and "What's hot in housing." You can look at home values in a given neighborhood. The site also has some fun with the latest news on celebrity homes. For instance, that Los Angeles house that Madonna bought for $13 million has "seven bedrooms, 15 bathrooms, a screening room, a library, a gym, a sauna, two guesthouses, a tennis court, a steam room and swimming pool."

Looking for Lenders

Literally thousands of mortgage lenders and brokers promote their products on the Internet. But surfer beware. When you are looking at these "fantastic offers," remember the old saying: If it sounds too good to be true, it probably is.

At the same time, one of the best ways to keep up with the latest mortgage rates and get solid home-buying advice is through many lenders' web sites. There are hundreds of these web sites. Here are just a few of them.

WELLS FARGO

Wells Fargo is the nation's largest mortgage lender. Its web site, www.wellsfargo.com, provides detailed advice on home buying and mortgages, whether you end up getting a mortgage from Wells Fargo or not. You can shop for homes across the country or down the street. With its "Home Loan Workbench," you can get loan recommendations tailored to your specific needs.

WASHINGTON MUTUAL

At the web site of Washington Mutual, the nation's second-biggest mortgage lender (www.washingtonmutual.com), you can find a variety of mortgage information. One useful feature is its calculator, "Which Loans & Rates Are Best for Me?" Plug in your numbers to compare different loan choices and rates.

BANK OF AMERICA

This bank's web site, www.bankofamerica.com, is an example of the kind of guidance you can find on many lenders' web sites. You can search mortgage rates, find home builders, and get a house-hunting checklist and a budget planning checklist. You can even look through bank-owned properties that are up for sale across the country.

COUNTRYWIDE FINANCIAL

At this national lender's web site, www.countrywide.com, you'll find such usable features as "A Step by Step Guide for First Time Home Buyers" and "Understanding the Loan Process."

LENDER COMPETITION

At such web sites as www.lendingtree.com and www.pickmy-mortgage, you can have lenders compete for your mortgage business. Lending Tree, for instance, sends your loan request to up to four lenders. They make their best offers, and you pick the one that you think is best for you.

MORTGAGE 101

For a good overview of current mortgage rates, plus a wide variety of mortgage tools, check www.mortgage101.com. Its offerings range from guides on "How Do I Get the Best Rates" and "How Do I Choose the Right Loan Program" to "Learn About the Mortgage Process," including "the first date with a broker."

Read All about It

Most newspapers and magazines have online versions, and these often provide consumer information, including advice on housing and real estate. Not only do these sites offer housing databases, but many provide articles on home buying and housing trends in understandable language. Here are just a few of them.

BUSINESSWEEK

This McGraw-Hill publication serves up housing advice on its www.businessweek.com web site. Click on the Investing and Personal Finance icons, and you'll be in the homes section. There you'll find advice on everything from "Deciding to buy or rent" and "Types of mortgage loans" to "Searching for a home" and "Negotiating a lower price."

THE WALL STREET JOURNAL

Part of the web site of this Dow Jones publication, www.wsj.com, is aimed at the upscale buyer. An example is its "Luxury-Home Index," which in late 2003 reported that a Washington, D.C., home "that cost $1.50 million in December 2002 is now, on average, valued at $1.64 million." But there are plenty of good data and home-buying computer tools for the rest of us. You can also go to its www.journalrealestate.com site for even more information, including articles that explain the current ins and outs of home sales trends. One caveat: Unlike most newspaper web sites, the *Wall Street Journal* site is available only to paid online subscribers.

SMART MONEY

The Web site for *Smart Money* magazine, another Dow Jones publication, at www.smartmoney.com, is one of the best consumer sites around. And its housing information is free. *Smart Money's* advice comes in no-nonsense language. Consider the "Home Buying Primer," which asks the question:

"How do I figure out which type of loan makes sense?"
The answer to the first question is easy enough: Mortgage products proliferate because lenders, hungry for business, are trying to rope you in any way they can. That certainly makes mortgage shopping confusing, but it also means you can probably find a mortgage tailor-made to meet your needs. **What Kind of Loan Should I Get?** can help familiarize you with the different types of loans available and which might be right for you.

KIPLINGER'S MAGAZINE

This consumer magazine has an online version at www.kiplinger.com. Its housing advice includes a "Home Buyer's Survival Kit." As the site explains: "This tutorial was designed to help you get the most out of buying a home, whether you're a first-time buyer, moving up or downsizing, we'll walk you through the steps and strategies you'll need." And it does so with such steps as "Choose a Broker," "Begin Your Search," "Make the Offer," and "Close the Deal."

CNN-MONEY

The cable TV network CNN and *Money* magazine have teamed up to offer the financial web site www.cnnmoney.com, which contains a section on real estate and home buying. Click on "Your Money" and you'll find such features as "Home prices, market by market" and "America's hottest zip codes." You can fantasize over photos of "Dream Homes," or get down to realty and click on "Homes for sale in your area."

LOCAL NEWSPAPERS

Most newspapers now have separate web sites where you can not only see what is in the printed paper but also get extra features. These sites are a good place to check for data and feature stories on the housing market in your areas. Robert J. Bruss is a knowledgeable national real estate columnist who answers specific questions in his "Real Estate Mailbag" column. Sometimes called the "Dear Abby of real estate," he also offers tips on home buying and ownership on his web site at www.bobbruss.com.

These sites only scratch the surface of what's available on real estate on the Web. But now it's time to go beyond virtual home tours to real ones.

CHAPTER 5

Something Old or Something New

Existing Houses versus New Houses

Should you buy a new home or an existing home? This is a decision that only you can make. Many people think that older homes have more charm than new ones. Older homes are in more established neighborhoods, with their own characteristics, whereas in most cases new homes are way out, without some of the features of a neighborhood. In addition, typically there are as many as 50 times more existing homes on the market than new ones at any given time. So the pick of existing homes is broader. Resale homes are typically 10 percent to 15 percent less expensive than new homes.

Other people prefer new homes, where everything is brand new: new appliances, new design, and new amenities that often aren't available in older homes. New homes tend to use more modern architecture and systems, are usually easier to maintain, and may be more energy-efficient. Typical new homes are bigger than typical older homes. Between 1972 and 2002, the average living space of new homes doubled from 1189 square feet to 2320 square feet (see Table 5-1). Some new homes are

Table 5-1 Cost Breakdown of Single-Family Home, 1972 and 2002

	1972		2002	
Hard cost	$13,188	54.3%	$95,100	50.83%
Land	4,925	20.2	$43,900	23.48
Financing	1,580	6.5	$ 3,985	2.13
Overhead and profit	2,940	12.3	$27,130	14.50
Other costs	1,667	6.7	$16,985	9.06
Total	$24,300	100.0%	$187,100	100.00%
Living area (sq. ft.)	1,189		2,114	+77.8%
Lot size (sq. ft.)	12,839		12,910	+0.5%
Lot cost per SF	$0.48		$3.40	+608.0%

Source: National Association of Home Builders.

much bigger and fancier than that, prompting complaints about "McMansions."

Despite the rising cost of land and government regulations, many new homes are priced competitively with existing homes. For instance, for a new house selling for $298,000 in 2003, the cost of land accounted for $70,000, or about 23 percent of the price, compared with 13 percent of the price in 1972. The cost per square foot to develop land rose to $3.40 from 48 cents three decades before.

Home builders have been able to keep prices under control, mainly through improved productivity. That's better than the cost-saving method one builder used when Mike Sumichrast was starting in the business many years ago.

A new home or an existing home? That's up to you. All we can do is point out some of the pros and cons to help you decide.

Advantages of a Newly Built Home

Here are the pluses of a new home as seen through the experienced eyes of Jeff Urban, who was president of the Greater Toronto Builders' Association in 1999:

Mike's Favorite Cost-Saving Story

On my first home-building job in the United States, near Trenton, New Jersey, I decided that we needed some more tools. In a nice friendly fashion, I suggested to my superior from New York, Sid Herman, that we go and buy these items. Sid looked at me horrified, and then called our people together. "Now listen, you guys. Mike here just came in and suggested that we go and *buy* some of the tools we need, such as brooms, shovels, rakes, and hammers."

And they started to laugh. And Sid, with his big, fat belly, was jumping up and down. He nearly choked from laughing so hard. They all laughed, screamed, and jumped up and down.

"What's so funny?" I asked Sid.

"What's so funny?" he asked. "*He* is asking *me* what's so funny?"

"If you want something, my boy, you go and *steal* it," was Sid's reply.

- You can get a contemporary floor plan that reflects the way you live today, not the way your grandparents lived 50 years ago.
- You can get new building materials and appliances that will last longer.
- You may earn instant equity. It's likely in today's market that homes in subsequent phases will sell for more.
- You can get what you want—now. Buyers can customize production homes as never before, selecting from a vast number of options and upgrades.
- Your operating costs will be much lower. New homes cost much less to operate than existing homes, thanks to energy codes implemented in the last 15 years.
- You can get great design for the money. The best production homes built today look far better than production

homes built in the 1950s, 1960s, and 1970s—the homes that people are now buying and trying to remodel. (See Figure 5-1.)

- You can gain access to valuable lifestyle amenities. You may have a walking or jogging trail outside your home. There may be tennis courts or open space for the kids to play nearby. You may even get a golf course membership with your new home.
- You can get a wired home. The advanced telephone wire and video cable in many new homes allows you to work at home every bit as conveniently as you work at the office. It would cost you thousands of dollars to retrofit an existing home in this fashion.
- You can live where no one has lived before. Everything around you is new, just as when you buy a new car. No one has used your bathrooms. There are no nasty smells in the basement.

Figure 5-1　A Newly Built Home

Photo by Anthony Traub.
Source: Builder Magazine.

DESIGN TRENDS

New homes offer the latest designs. Gopal Ahluwalia, director of research for the National Association of Home Builders, notes the trends:

- The average size of a new house has stabilized at 2320 square feet over the last few years, and we expect it to remain in this range.
- The biggest change over the last few years is that 9-foot or higher ceilings are becoming a standard feature in the average home. It had been 8 feet.
- Median lot size is also declining because of growth controls. The median lot size is just below 9000 square feet. It's dropped slowly in the last 10 years, from 10,000 square feet.
- People want more special features and more quality, such as high-end appliances and structured wiring known as "CAT 5" wiring, as well as low-maintenance materials.
- Larger kitchens adjacent to family rooms are getting more emphasis. And bathrooms are getting larger, with upgraded features.
- Living rooms are disappearing or shrinking, and the number one priority among specialty rooms is a laundry room.
- Heated flooring as well as heated driveways are being used, where you push a button and it melts the snow.

There are scores of national and local builders, offering an endless variety of new homes. For just one example, Centex is building homes in 54 markets in the United States. In Orlando, Florida, for example, Centex offers over 75 home plans in 18 communities, with several new communities planned. Home designs range from 1434 square feet to 3541 square feet. Homes are priced from the $90,000s to more than $300,000. Other major home builders include Pulte, Lennar, KB Home, D.R. Horton, NVR, Ryland, Del Webb, Toll Brothers, and

Table 5-2 Top 15 Home Builders
(by annual revenues)

1. Centex Corp., www.centex.com
2. Pulte Homes, www.pulte.com
3. D.R. Horton, www.drhort.com.lennar.com
4. Lennar Corp., www.lennar.com
5. KB Home, www.kbhome.com
6. NVR, www.nvrinc.com
7. The Ryland Group, www.ryland.com
8. Beazer Homes USA, www.beazer.com
9. Hovnanian Enterprises, www.khov.com
10. Toll Brothers, www.tollbrothers.com
11. M.D.C. Holdings, www.richmondamerican.com
12. Standard Pacific Corp., www.standardpacifichomes.com
13. Shea Homes, www.sheahomes.com
14. Weyerhauser Real Estate Co., www.weyerhauser.com
15. Technical Olympic USA, www.tousa.com

Source: Builder Magazine.

Ryan Homes. Table 5-2 gives the top 15 home builders by annual revenue.

Disadvantages of New Homes

There also are some possible downsides to buying a new home rather than buying an existing home.

- New homes are generally somewhat more expensive. In 2003, the median price of new homes was $194,100, compared with $170,000 for existing homes. By 2005, new homes are expected to reach a median of $226,000, while prices of existing homes should increase to $196,000.
- Lots are typically smaller for new homes. Lot sizes have not changed much, if at all, being about 13,000 square feet. It's

hard to find a home with an acre or two of land in the new subdivisions, although there are some.

- It would be rather unusual to find any kind of mature land-scaping in a new subdivision.
- Very few new homes offer the luxury of a fenced yard. Typically new homes have open landscaping with no fences.
- If the new house is in a development, you may have to put up with construction work all around you for a while.
- A new development doesn't have the character that an old subdivision does.
- Many new homes are not entirely trouble-free. Like any new product, a new home has to be lived in to discover some of the problems. You may have to keep bugging them, but most builders will fix problems for up to a year. You can usually get a warranty to cover problems that surface later.

The most frequent major complaints about new homes turn up in six major categories: (1) leaky roofs, (2) leaky basements, (3) finish defects, such as carpentry, moldings, trim, cabinets, and so on, (4) plumbing problems, (5) defective doors and windows, and (6) miscellaneous defects, such as chipped sinks, loose doorknobs, or loose or not properly fitted carpeting.

Perhaps the most irritating problem for buyers of new homes is the builder's failure to finish all the little things—and sometimes the big things—that the buyer was promised. Sometimes the house itself isn't even completed anywhere near when the salesperson promised it would be. There is always a struggle between the construction workers and the salespeople.

As a former construction superintendent, Mike Sumichrast knows full well that the finished work depends on dozens of subcontractors. If one subcontractor doesn't finish the job, the second subcontractor in line cannot start its job. You must have a floor before you can start laying floor tiles. And then there is the weather. If it keeps pouring for 2 weeks, your chances of doing outside work are zilch.

What can you do to protect yourself from such headaches? To be on the safe side, if you are selling a current house, plan with the understanding that the move-in date for your new home will probably be later than the salesperson says. Ask for a provision in your new-home contract stating that the builders will give you at least 30 days' notice before the closing date on the house so that you can plan to move.

When you sell your old house, leave leeway in your sales contract for a move-out date. If possible, include a provision allowing you to rent your old house for a time after you sell it.

More Things to Check

- Find out what you will *really* be paying for the house. New houses are sold at a base price, but like new cars, they come with lots of options or "upgrades," such as better carpeting, fancier faucets, and built-in bookcases. The costs of these upgrades aren't always disclosed up front, and they can add up fast. Often, you can get these things cheaper by having them done by somebody else after you move in.
- Before you buy a new house, make sure that the builder is not planning to bulldoze the land behind your back fence to put in another group of houses, or to put a shopping center in the vacant land across from your house and change the beautiful view you think you will enjoy. This is a particular problem in a town-house development or in the first group of condos. Ask whether your view is legally protected.
- Check whether your kids can go to local schools. Your address doesn't necessarily qualify you to send your kids to the neighborhood schools. It is the school district your house belongs to that determines this.
- Check the street drainage system. Does it allow sufficient outflow of rainwater without flooding the street, and possibly your basement?

- Check on yard restrictions or whether you can build a fence around your property.

Finally, when you are shopping for a new house, look for signs of inferior workmanship. A key indicator is carpentry work. There are many things in a house that you will never notice, but most people can recognize sloppy carpentry—things like joints that don't fit, countertops with rough edges, and doors that don't close properly. These and other such items often indicate sloppy workmanship or poor supervision.

Before you go to settlement, you will have a chance to do a "walk-though" of the house to see what items still need to be completed or repaired before you take possession. The builder's representative will have a "punch list" of items in the house, showing what has been completed and what needs to be done. (It is called a punch list because the builder's representative punches each item when it is completed. Some buyers say that it is called a punch list because when they are see how many items are not completed, they feel like punching the builder in the nose.)

Since you're probably not a housing expert, you may need some expert help. Increasingly, as houses become larger and more expensive, buyers are hiring home-inspection services to check newly built houses as well as existing ones. You can have an inspector accompany you on the walk-through. Some builders don't like this idea, but you should have it written into the sales contract. Also make sure that the contract sets the walk-through several days before the final settlement so that you still have time to do something about getting deficiencies corrected.

Whether or not you have help, any deficiencies should be listed in detail on your punch list. Don't go to settlement unless (1) all of the items are completed, or (2) if they aren't, the builder agrees in writing to do the work within a specific time.

You can make one final check on the presettlement walk-through of your new home. Here is what the National Association of Home Builders says you should be looking for.

Figure 5-2 New House, Old Style

Photo by Anthony Traub.
Source: Builder Magazine.

Presettlement Walk-Through Checklist

Grading

- Does the ground around the foundation slope away from the house?
- Make sure that the water does not pond in swales. To check, water the areas with a hose, if possible.
- Are there signs of erosion?
- Is the shrubbery placed at least 2 to 3 feet from the foundation?

- If the house has a basement, are the basement window wells clean and graveled?

Roof and Gutters

- Are the shingles flat and tight?
- Is the flashing securely in place?
- Do the gutters, downspouts, and splash blocks direct water away from the house?

Exterior Appearance

- Are the windows and doors sealed and protected by weatherstripping?
- Are the trim and fittings tight? Are there any cracks?
- Does the paint cover the surface and trim smoothly?
- Has landscaping been installed according to the terms of your contract?

Doors and Windows

- Are all doors and windows sealed?
- Do they open and close easily?
- Is the glass properly in place? Is any of the glass loose or cracked?

Finishes

- Is the painting satisfactory in all rooms, closets, and stairways?
- Did the painters miss any spots?
- Are the trim and moldings in place?

Floors

- Is the carpet tight? Do the seams match?
- Are there any ridges or seam gaps in vinyl tile or linoleum?
- Are wooden floors properly finished?

Appliances, Fixtures, Surfaces, Etc.

- Do all of the appliances operate properly?
- Are all of the appliances the model and color you ordered?
- Check all faucets and plumbing fixtures, including toilets and showers, to make sure they operate properly.
- Check all electrical fixtures and outlets. Bring a hair dryer to test the outlets.
- Do the heating, cooling, and water-heating units operate properly? Test them to make sure.
- If the home has a fireplace, do the draft and damper work?
- Are there any nicks, scratches, cracks, or burns on any surfaces, including cabinets and countertops?
- Test the doorbell. Also test the intercom system, garage door opener, and any other optional items.

Basement and Attic

- Are there indications of dampness or leaks?
- Is there significant cracking in the floors or foundation walls?
- Are there any obvious defects in exposed components, such as floor joists, I-beams, support columns, insulation, heating ducts, plumbing, electrical, and so on?

Certificate of Occupancy

- Has your local municipality signed off on your house?

Source: www.nahb.org: The NAHB adds: "Some problems may not be readily apparent during the walk-through. Even a professional inspector might miss a few. Most warranties cover any such problems that are the result of faulty workmanship. However, warranties usually exclude problems that result from owner neglect or improper maintenance."

Advantages of Existing Homes

Some people prefer older houses to what they view as the cookie-cutter homes of new-home subdivisions. Existing homes can offer some potential advantages:

- The neighborhood may have more character. There may be a wider variety of housing styles than in a new subdivision.
- For the same price, you can generally get a little more size when buying an existing home than when buying a new one.
- You may get more land.
- Older homes may have mature trees, gardens, a fenced yard, or a pool.
- In many instances you may be able to move into an existing home much sooner than into a new home.
- You know what the neighborhood is like. It is also likely to be closer to the city instead of far out in a newly developed subdivision.
- The value of an existing home is already well established.
- Property taxes are well known and have been established over a longer period of time.
- You don't have to wait until the house is built. If you are in a hurry, your best choice may be an existing home.
- Chances are that an older home will require less commuting time than a new home.

Disadvantages of Existing Homes

The biggest disadvantage of buying an existing home is the potential cost of repairs. The items needing repair can run the gamut of all the items found in a house, from the electrical, plumbing, heating, and air-conditioning systems, to all the appliances, the paint job, and so on.

- What will happen to the area is always an unknown. Is it going to remain steady, or will it deteriorate? The chances for a decline are always greater in an older area than in a new one.
- A home warranty is not as readily available for an older home as for a new home.
- In an older home, you may have to face not only immediate repairs, but also the need for an update. Who is happy with

a 20-year-old kitchen? What about the bathrooms? The deteriorating driveway? The falling roof shingles?
- The garden may have been a selling point to your spouse, but what about the 30-year-old trees falling all over the place, including onto your precious roof?

Most older homes—and by that we mean homes that are more than 30 years old—do have problems and need to be checked out. The most important part of the house to check is the basic structure. Consider getting a reputable home-inspection or engineering firm to give you a full report on the condition of the house. It can tell you what specific repairs are needed, and whether the repairs are worth making.

You can make your own assessment of the house's conditions by following this short outline of some of the basic problems found in older homes.

1. *Water.* This is a very common problem in older homes. Often it is a result of poor gutter alignment, poor downspout direction, and/or poor surface grading. Water can be detected by looking for discoloration of the floor tile, stained paneling at floor level, dark spots on cinder block, and similar other signs in the basement.
2. *Plumbing.* In older homes, pressure tends to drop substantially because of rusty galvanized pipes. Replacement of these pipes is a major expense in older homes. Test for leaks and water pressure. A leak in lead waste piping cannot be patched. If the bathroom is remodeled, lead pipes must be replaced.
3. *Termite activity.* A combination of wood, dirt, darkness, and dampness will bring termites. The problem is particularly acute if there is a crawl space with dirt very close to wood floor joists.
4. *Roofs.* The roofs of older homes may have water leaks. Check metal roofs for rust, tile roofs for rusting, and built-up roofs with gravel for spongy spaces and bubbles.

5. *Retaining walls.* Large cracks sometimes form, which usually indicates that surface water is collecting behind the wall, freezing, and causing pressure. This can be demonstrative of poor construction work.

6. *Interior walls and ceilings.* Most older homes have plaster on wood lath. Over the years, the wood lath strips lose resilience and pull away from the joists and studs, causing waves in walls and ceilings. Wood lath is very sensitive to moisture.

7. *Electric wiring.* Most older homes have inadequate wiring. Usually there are only one or two outlets per room, and this does not meet many codes. Most newer homes have outlets installed every 12 feet. Replacing wiring can be costly, but it also could save your life.

8. *Insulation.* Older homes are not as well insulated as newer ones. In particular, there may be a lack of insulation between masonry walls and interior walls.

9. *Appliances.* Older homes do not have the variety or the quality of appliances that newer ones do. Given technological changes, newer and better appliances are available to consumers.

10. *Windows.* Older homes usually have windows that readily conduct cold air into the house. Replacement of these windows is expensive.

The main difference between a new home and an existing home is that in an older home, you need to factor in the cost of necessary repairs. If you are considering buying an older house, look at Table 5-3, which shows the approximate expected life of many major components of a house. Use the list to determine how soon you might expect major repair bills. You'll especially want to check big-ticket items such as the furnace, the central air conditioning, and the roof, each of which can cost you $5000 to $10,000. Kitchen appliances, washer, and dryer also could be on their last legs.

Table 5-3 Things That Wear Out and Go "Ouch" in the Pocketbook:
Life Expectancy of Various Parts of the House

Life Expectancy of Household Components	
Appliances	**Life in Years**
Compactors	10
Dishwashers	10
Dryers	14
Disposal	10
Freezers, compact	12
Freezers, standard	16
Microwave ovens	11
Electric ranges	17
Gas ranges	19
Gas ovens	14
Refrigerators, compact	14
Refrigerators, standard	17
Washers, automatic and compact	13
Exhaust fans	20
Source: Appliance Statistical Review, April 1990.	
Bathrooms	**Life in Years**
Cast iron bathtubs	50
Fiberglass bathtub and showers	10–15
Shower doors, average quality	25
Toilets	50
Sources: Neil Kelly Designers, Thompson House of Kitchens and Bath.	
Cabinetry	**Life in Years**
Kitchen cabinets	15–20
Medicine cabinets and bath vanities	20
Sources: Kitchen Cabinet Manufacturers Association, Neil Kelly Designers.	

Table 5-3 (Continued)

Closet Systems	Life in Years
Closet shelves	Lifetime
Countertops	**Life in Years**
Laminate	10–15
Ceramic tile, high-grade installation	Lifetime
Wood/butcher block	20+
Granite	20+
Sources: AFPAssociates of Western Plastics, Ceramic Tile Institute of America.	
Doors	**Life in Years**
Screen	25–50
Interior, hollow core	Less than 30
Interior, solid core	30–lifetime
Exterior, protected overhang	80–100
Exterior, unprotected and exposed	25–30
Folding	30–lifetime
Garage doors	20–50
Garage door opener	10
Sources: Wayne Dalton Corporation, National Wood Window and Door Association, Raynor Garage Doors.	
Electrical	**Life in Years**
Copper wiring, copper plated, copper-clad aluminum, and bare copper	100+
Armored cable (BX)	Lifetime
Conduit	Lifetime
Source: Jesse Aronstein, Engineering Consultant.	
Finishes Used for Waterproofing	**Life in Years**
Paint, plaster, and stucco	3–5
Sealer, silicone, and waxes	1–5
Source: Brick Institute of America.	

(continued)

Table 5-3 (Continued)

Floors	Life in Years
Oak or pine	Lifetime
Slate flagstone	Lifetime
Vinyl sheet or tile	20–30
Terrazzo	Lifetime
Carpeting (depends on installation, amount of traffic, and quality of carpet)	11
Marble (depends on installation, thickness of marble, and amount of traffic)	Lifetime+

Sources: Carpet and Rug Institute, Congoleum Corporation, Hardwood Plywood Manufacturers Association, Marble Institute, National Terrazzo and Mosaic Association, National Wood Flooring Association, Resilient Floor Covering Institute.

Footings and Foundation	Life in Years
Poured footings and foundations	200
Concrete block	100
Cement	50
Waterproofing, bituminous coating	10
Termite proofing (may have shorter life in damp climates)	5

Source: WR Grace and Company.

Heating, Ventilation, and Air Conditioning (HVAC)	Life in Years
Central air conditioning unit (newer units should last longer)	15
Window Unit	10
Air conditioner compressor	15
Humidifier	8
Electric water heater	14
Gas water heater (depends on type of water heater lining and quality of water)	11–13
Forced-air furnaces, heat pump	15

Table 5-3 (Continued)

Rooftop air conditioners	15
Boilers, hot water or steam (depends on quality of water)	30
Furnaces, gas- or oil-fired	18
Unit heaters, gas or electric	13
Radiant heaters, electric	10
Radiant heaters, hot water or steam	25
Baseboard systems	20
Diffusers, grilles, and registers	27
Induction and fan coil units	20
Dampers	20
Centrifugal fans	25
Axial fans	20
Ventilating roof-mounted fans	20
DX, water, and steam coils	20
Electric coils	15
Heat exchangers, shell-and-tube	24
Molded insulation	20
Pumps, sump and well	10
Burners	21

Sources: Air Conditioning and Refrigeration Institute, *Air Conditioning, Heating, and Refrigeration News,* Air Movement and Control Association, American Gas Association, American Society of Gas Engineers, American Society of Heating, Refrigeration and Air-Conditioning Engineers, Inc., Safe Aire Incorporated.

Home Security Appliances	**Life in Years**
Intrusion systems	14
Smoke detectors	12
Smoke/fire/intrusion systems	10

Insulation	**Life in Years**
For foundations, roofs, ceilings, walls, and floors	Lifetime

Sources: Insulation Contractors Association of America, North American Insulation Manufacturers Association.

(continued)

Table 5-3 (Continued)

Landscaping	Life in Years
Wooden decks	15
Brick and concrete patios	24
Tennis courts	10
Concrete walks	24
Gravel walks	4
Asphalt driveways	10
Swimming pools	18
Sprinkler systems	12
Fences	12

Sources: Associated Landscape Contractors of America, Irrigation Association.

Masonry	Life in Years
Chimney, fireplace, and brick veneer	Lifetime
Brick and stone walls	100+
Stucco	Lifetime

Sources: Brick Institute of America, Architectural Components, National Association of Brick Distributors, National Stone Association.

Millwork	Life in Years
Stairs, trim	50–100
Disappearing stairs	30–40

Paints and Stains	Life in Years
Exterior paint on wood, brick, and aluminum	7–10
Interior wall paint (depends on the acrylic content)	5–10
Interior trim and door paint	5–10
Wallpaper	7

Sources: Finnaren and Haley, Glidden Company, The Wall Paper.

Table 5-3 *(Continued)*

Plumbing	Life in Years
Waste piping, cast iron	75–100
Sinks, enamel steel	5–10
Sinks, enamel cast iron	25–30
Sinks, china	25–30
Faucets, low quality	13–15
Faucets, high quality	15–20

Sources: American Concrete Pipe Association, Cast Iron Soil and Pipe Institute, Neil Kelly Designers, Thompson House of Kitchens and Baths.

Roofing	Life in Years
Asphalt and wood shingles and shakes	15–30
Tile (depends on quality of tile and climate)	50
Slate (depends on grade)	50–100
Sheet metal (depends on gauge of metal and quality of fastening and application)	20–50+
Built-up roofing, asphalt	12–25
Built-up roofing, coal and tar	12–30
Asphalt composition shingle	15–30
Asphalt overlag	25–35

Source: National Roofing Contractors Association

Rough Structure	Life in Years
Basement floor systems	Lifetime
Framing, exterior and interior walls	Lifetime

Source: NAHB Research Foundation.

Shutters	Life in Years
Wood, interior	Lifetime
Wood, exterior (depends on weather conditions)	4–5
Vinyl plastic, exterior	7–8
Aluminum, interior	35–50
Aluminum, exterior	3–5

Sources: A.C. Shutters, Inc., Alcoa Building Products, American Heritage Shutters.

(continued)

Table 5-3 (*Continued*)

Siding	Life in Years
Gutters and downspouts	30
Siding, wood (depends on maintenance)	10–100
Siding, steel	50–Lifetime
Siding, aluminum	20–50
Siding, vinyl	50

Sources: Alcoa Building Products, Alside, Inc., Vinyl Siding Institute.

Walls and Window Treatments	Life in Years
Drywall and plaster	30–70
Ceramic tile, high grade installation	Lifetime

Sources: Association of Wall and Ceiling Industries International, Ceramic Tile Institute of America.

Windows	Life in Years
Window glazing	20
Wood casement	20–50
Aluminum and vinyl casement	20–30
Screen	25–50

Sources: Best Built Products, Optimum Window Manufacturing, Safety Glazing Certification Council, Screen Manufacturers Association.

Source: Copyright © 1993 by National Association of Home Builders, originally published in *Housing Economics,* August 1993.

The material in Table 5-3 was developed for the National Association of Home Builders (NAHB) Economics Department based on a survey of manufacturers, trade associations, and product researchers. Many factors affect the life expectancy of housing components and need to be considered when making replacement decisions, including the quality of the components, the quality of their installation, their level of maintenance, weather and climatic conditions, and the intensity of their use. Some components remain functional but become obsolete because of changing styles and tastes or because of product improvements. The life expectancy estimates in the table are provided largely by the industries or manufacturers that make and sell the components listed.

CHAPTER 6

Shopping for a Good Buy—from the Outside

Approaches to House Hunting

House hunting can take many forms. One approach is to look in the newspapers or on the Internet, find some houses that look good to you, no matter where in your area they are, and go look at them.

A better way is to first decide where you really want to live, *then* go find the best buy you can get in that area. Find a neighborhood where the living is easy, the schools are good, the commuting is at least tolerable, and you will feel at home.

How do you find a good buy in an area in which you want to live? Let us count the ways.

NOSE INTO THE NEIGHBORHOOD

The number one reason for picking a house is the neighborhood in which it is located, according to several surveys over time by the National Association of Home Builders. One poll indicated that the second most important factor is proximity to work. Other factors are closeness to relatives, convenience to shopping and transportation, and a low tax rate.

Since this is probably not the last home you will ever live in, you need to consider another key factor: price appreciation. Will you be able to sell your house for more than you paid for it? Chances are that you will, if your house is in the right neighborhood.

The three most important features of a house are location, location, and location, according to an old saying in real estate. And it's true, true, true. Location and the character of the neighborhood largely determine the value of a home.

Looks can be deceiving. A fancy house in a declining neighborhood isn't a good buy. But a plain place in an up-and-coming area can turn into a fancy investment. It could pay you to spend more money and buy a house in a superior area rather than buying in an area of inexpensive homes without much hope of a strong resale value.

One way to tell if an area is a growth area is to find out what houses in the neighborhood were selling for a couple of years ago and compare it with current selling prices. This gives you an idea of what appreciation has occurred and whether values are still rising. In the old days, you usually had to make a trip down to the county courthouse to get this information. Today, in many areas of the country, these data are available from county records on the Internet. Remember to compare past selling prices with current *selling* prices. That is, find out what houses are actually selling for, not what the asking price is.

LEARN ABOUT SCHOOLS

Even if you don't have children, educate yourself about the school system. Remember, you're not just buying a house; you're also making an investment. So think about how the house, which you haven't even bought yet, will appeal to future buyers who do have kids.

Parents will pay almost anything to get a house in a prestige school district. "The first question that prospective home buyers ask is where their children will go to school," said one real estate agent in Maryland. "Then they want to know how that school system compares with other schools in the county."

If you're a parent, or plan to be, that should be your first question, too. The problem is how to get honest answers. Real estate agents aren't supposed to give their opinion on whether the local schools are good or bad, especially if they are bad. However, housing ads that innocently state that a house is in a specific school district are a sure sign that the area's schools are in demand.

Local school officials probably won't be much help, either. Their school is always good. Nevertheless, it's a good idea to visit local schools. For one thing, you'll be able to check the outward appearance of the school and its facilities to see if it seems up-to-date or on the decline. In talking to school officials, you also can get information on average class sizes, how student compare with those at other schools on standardized achievement tests, and what special courses and counseling are available. Fortunately, a lot of this information is now available on the Internet.

Even in good schools, such as those in Montgomery County, Maryland, outside of Washington, D.C., you can't let the bureaucrats push you around.

CHECK THE CRIME RATE

Make sure that the crime rate in a neighborhood isn't sneaking up before you make a commitment to move there. Nothing can send real estate values down faster than newspaper and TV stories about a neighborhood crime wave. Local papers often publish police reports on calls in various areas. Or check with local police officials. For national trends, you can check the FBI web site.

In most residential areas, your main concern is about burglaries. Crime varies widely from area to area and in different parts of the country. According to one survey by Morgan Quitno Press, a Lawrence, Kansas–based publishing and research company, the safest cities in America are Amherst, New York; Brick Township, New Jersey; and Newton, Massachusetts. The most

Mike's Favorite School Story

Several years after my wife, Marika, died, I married a Czech woman from Prague, Eva. She had a 12-year-old daughter, Katerina. Neither one spoke English. While Eva attended a private school to learn English, we hired a girl next door to help Katerina with her reading during the summer of 1990. Then we enrolled Kata in public secondary school in an ESOL class. (ESOL is a class for English for speakers of other languages.) After a few days, we received a rejection note from the school, saying that they could not accept her because she had been living in Potomac for just a few months, not enough to establish a residency. That got me pretty mad.

The next day I went to the school to talk to the principal. I said, "We have been living in this house for over 28 years and paid a bundle of property taxes. In all those years we have never sent any of our three boys to public schools. They all attended private schools. And now you mean to tell me that you will not accept Katerina in ESOL class? I will see about that!" I slapped my fist on the table and left. It worked. She was accepted by the school the same day.

Postscript. Katerina got nothing but straight A's. After high school at Churchill, she enrolled as a University of Maryland exchange student at Peking University, China, and graduated from Maryland with honors in 2000. She began working full time at the U.S. Treasury in Washington, D.C, while getting her master's degree in criminology.

dangerous cities are St. Louis, Missouri; Detroit, Michigan; and Atlanta, Georgia. See Table 6-1.

Obviously, you want to avoid neighborhoods that are known for violent crimes. As of 2003, the city with the dubious distinction of having the highest murder rate was Washington, D.C., followed

Table 6-1 Top 10 Safest and Most Dangerous Cities

Rank	Safest	Most Dangerous
1	Amherst, NY	St. Louis, MO
2	Brick Township, NJ	Detroit, MI
3	Newton, MA	Atlanta, GA
4	Thousand Oaks, CA	Gary, IN
5	Sunnyvale, CA	Baltimore, MD
6	Cary, NC	Camden, NJ
7	Orem, UT	Compton, CA
8	Clarkstown, NY	Flint, MI
9	Mission Viejo, CA	Tampa, FL
10	Lake Forest, CA	Jackson, MS
By Size	**Safest**	**Most Dangerous**
Small	Brick Township, NJ	Camden, NJ
Medium	Amherst, NY	St. Louis, MO
Large	San Jose, CA	Detroit, MI

Source: Morgan Quitno Press, www.morganquitno.com, Lawrence, KS.

by Detroit, Michigan. Of course, even these cities have plenty of safe neighborhoods.

CHECK THE COMMUTE

How far do you want to travel to work? How congested are the roads if you drive? Is public transportation available?

Don't take anybody's word for it. Once you zero in on an area, drive to your job and back through rush-hour traffic. Check the bus, subway, or train schedules. How often do they run, and how long would it take you to get to work?

Make sure you are comfortable with the commuting time. Again we stress: Remember that future buyers will also want convenient transportation. That is one reason that a close-in location with good access to transportation adds to the value of your home. How maddening your commute is depends on where you live. According to a study by Sperling's www.Bestplaces.net, the nation's least drivable city is Los Angeles, followed by San Francisco. If you want an easy car commute, move to Corpus Christi, Texas, or Brownsville, Texas. (See Table 6-2.)

Table 6-2 Ten Most and Least Drivable Cities

Ten Most Drivable Cities, 2003	Ten Least Drivable Cities, 2003
1. Corpus Christi, TX	1. Los Angeles, CA
2. Brownsville, Harlingten, TX	2. San Francisco, CA
3. Beaumont–Port Arthur, TX	3. Chicago, IL
4. Pensacola, FL	4. Denver, CO
5. Fort Myers–Cape Coral, FL	5. Boston, MA
6. Oklahoma City, OK	6. Oakland, CA
7. Birmingham, AL	7. Detroit, MI
8. El Paso, TX	8. New York, NY
9. Memphis, TN	9. Seattle–Bellevue, Everett, WA
10. Tulsa, OK	10. Washington, DC

Source: Sperling's BestPlaces.Net, www.bestplaces.net.

LOCATION AND CONVENIENCE

You probably don't want to live next door to the supermarket. But at the same time, you don't want to make an all-day excursion just to pick up a loaf of bread. Check the distance to grocery stores, shopping areas, gas stations, theaters, and recreation facilities. If you have young children who are interested in sports, find out if there is Little League baseball, soccer, or other facilities in the area. See if there is a health club, gym, or recreational club nearby that you could join, and how much it costs.

BACK TO THE FUTURE

When you focus in on an area, take an even closer look at the future. Anticipate changes that could dramatically change the value of your house, for better or worse.

As a home buyer, you're mainly interested in the near future, say 3 to 10 years. But that may be long enough for the community to change. What kind of change can you expect?

On the negative side, there is the possibility of deterioration. The physical look of the houses on the street is one clue. Are the houses well kept, or are they starting to look rundown? If the community is 30 years old, it could have lost some of its zip. If the present owners aren't modernizing their homes, future buyers may look elsewhere and the market could decline. But if houses are being improved and people are moving into the area, the neighborhood can be born again.

Are changes planned that would affect the neighborhood? "In discussing residential data with our residential appraisers, we agreed that one of the most overlooked, but important neighborhood items to consider is the surroundings and use," said one real estate agent in Manassas, Virginia. "This is particularly important when the property adjoining the house is undeveloped. Far too often a person purchases next to a wooded lot for privacy or buys a home because of an attractive view and six months later is dismayed to find bulldozers clearing trees from surrounding land, or a town house project that blocks the view he wanted."

"There would be fewer disappointments if the buyer of a property would take the time to check with public officials for proposed future development surrounding the property," she said.

That is exactly what you should do. Check with your local planning commission. Look at plans for future highways. A roadway that cuts the neighborhood in half could hurt values. However, a new expressway nearby that will speed the commute may add to its appeal. Future expansion of transportation services, such as a subway, could push up values.

What other housing developments are planned for your area? Are they rental developments, condominiums, or single-family homes? Will they add to or detract from the appeal of the community? What about commercial construction and future congestion?

To save you running around, you can try the services of the Internet. You may be surprised at what you can find out—just about everything.

House Shopping

Once you have an idea of where you want to buy, it's time to start looking in specific areas. There are some basic strategies.

THE LONE RANGER APPROACH

You can do the shopping without professional help. Check newspaper want ads for houses in the area. Don't pay much attention to the claims. "Won't last long at this price!" probably just means it's so overpriced that the seller will have to lower the price soon. And of course, the ads leave out the bad things. Look for homes in your price range with the features you want.

These days, you may even be able to shop by watching television. Some cities have stations that show houses for sale. And after you start looking at homes in person, you may think the For Sale signs are talking to you. In fact, they may be. Some signs have a low-power transmitter that broadcasts a description of a home's selling points.

WORK WITH AN AGENT

The other way to shop is to find a faithful real estate agent companion. Good agents know the area and what houses are available. They have access to the Multiple Listing Service, which provides information on houses being sold by other agencies. As a result, the number of potential homes that you can find out about from one agent is greatly multiplied. Agents also get an advance look at houses before they are placed on the market.

As we have discussed, these days you can get much of this information yourself on the Internet. The data are provided free of charge by www.Realtor.com and most real estate agencies.

A big advantage for you, the buyer, is that the agent's services are free. He or she collects all or part of the commission charged to the seller. On the other hand, that means that the agent's obligation is to the seller, not to you. So no matter how helpful an agent may be, don't share your bargaining strategy with that agent.

Buyer's Agent   If you want a real estate agent who will represent solely your interests, you can contact a buyer's agent. This agent will bargain for you based on your instructions and won't share confidential information with the seller. You don't pay this agent. Buyer's agents also collect part of the commission paid by the seller.

Most agents, whether or not they are buyer's agents, will try to provide you with fair service, knowing that good recommendations are the key to future sales. Most are members of major real estate associations, which have ethical standards. The two biggest associations are the National Association of Realtors and the National Association of Real Estate Agents. Table 6-3 lists the largest national real estate sellers.

Table 6-3 Largest National Real Estate Sellers

Century 21 Real Estate, www.century21.com
Coldwell Banker Real Estate, www.coldwellbanker.com
ERA Franchise Systems, www.eraonline.com
GMAC Home Services, www.gmacrealestate.com
Help-U-Sell Real Estate, www.helpusell.net
Keller-Williams Realty, www.kellerwilliams.com
Prudential Real Estate, www.prudential.com/realestate
Realty Executives International, www.realtyexecutives.com
Realty World, www.realtyworld.com
Re/Max International, www.remax.com
Weichert Realtors, www.weichert.com

Source: National Association of Realtors.

Whether you seek help or decide to go it alone, you want to check the neighborhoods yourself. Grab a good map, hop in your car, and make a windshield inspection of the area. Better, yet, walk around the neighborhood and talk to people who live there. Even if the neighborhood looks nice, there are other things to check.

What Style of House?

Houses come in different styles, shapes, and sizes. Some people like a stately, two-story colonial. Others are crazy about easy-living one-story ramblers. Some go for contemporaries. You need to ask yourself which style is best for your individual tastes and needs. The popularity of some styles waxes and wanes over time.

In terms of investment, style probably won't make much difference, unless you buy an oddball home sitting among conventional ones. Don't buy the only Spanish villa among two-story, red-brick colonials. Most buyers like traditional-looking homes. They don't go for wild, screaming colors and styles.

In short, stay away from extremes. Future buyers will, too.

Mike's Favorite Split-Level Story

After our dismal performance in 1955 with Cape Cod slab houses in Pennsylvania, our New York company bought a piece of land on Route 40 east in Columbus, Ohio. We were the first company in Columbus to build split-level houses. It was a huge success. In the first 3 weeks we sold 90 homes. Prices were from $15,990 to $18,425 with 4½ percent mortgages.

In the 1950s the split levels, the "modern era" homes of the time, accounted for nearly one-third of all new homes built. Their popularity declined to under 10 percent in 1980 and dropped out of sight to less than 1 percent in 2002. Nobody builds them any more.

Yet, in the area where I live, there are some of these relics, as there are all over the United States. They are no longer called "split levels"—they have been given the sexier name of "split foyers." But surprisingly they sell quite well because there are more expensive homes all around them, and the prices of these split "foyers" have moved up in line with other prices in the neighborhood.

The moral of the story: Location, for the most part, is what determines home prices.

Evaluating a House from the Outside

At last, you're looking at a real house in the area you have selected. This is what you should look for from the outside.

> *Quiet streets.* Keep your eyes and ears open as you head for your potential house. Look at the street. It can affect the value of your house. The best locations are dead-end streets that offer escape from traffic noise and congestion. Next are streets away from main intersections that aren't

Mike's Favorite House Design Story

In the early 1960s we started a new subdivision in Columbus, Ohio, with six models. The owner-builder, Ernest G. Fritsche, wanted us to build simply designed, inexpensive homes, which he knew would sell. We hade six models, and we tried to convince our brand-new architect that we knew what we were doing. But he was one of these young, hardheaded architects, and he would not budge. So Fritsche finally said, "Let him design one model." And he did. It was called a "Polynesian," and it was really a beautiful house, a ranch-type, slab (no basement), with a lot of light and a widely opened living area.

We had some 3000 potential customers coming through these model homes. We asked each one of them to fill out a card showing preferences among all six models. What can I tell you? The architect was right. Over one-half of the people who responded marked Polynesian as the best-liked model, the winner. We sold some two hundred homes in the first section. How many Polynesians did we sell? We sold one, the model. We sold it to the young, smart, aggressive, up-and-coming architect.

through streets with speeding cars. That means less worry for parents with small children or people with pets.

Before you decide to buy, check the area at night. In many places, the neighborhood undergoes a metamorphosis after dark. Make sure that your sleep won't be disturbed.

Garages. Is there a driveway, or will you have to park on the street in front of the house? A driveway and a garage, or at least a carport, adds to the value of your home. According to "Decisions for the 1990s," a study done for the National Association of Home Builders by Michael Sumichrast and Gopal Ahluwalia, most buyers want a garage. Two-thirds of potential buyers prefer to have a two-car garage, and 16 percent would like a three-car garage. The update done in 2002 shows pretty much the same results.

The lot: Look at the lay of the land. Is it well landscaped? Attractive lawns, shrubs, and trees increase the value. Look at the outside ground to make sure it slopes away from the house. It must take water away from the house, or the water will go inside. The condition of the gutters and downspouts is also a factor.

The yard. A big yard has big appeal for young couples who are raising children. As your kids grow up and stop playing around the house, the romance of a big yard can fade. You are left with lots of grass to mow and nobody to help you. And as the number of couples with families declines, big yards are declining in popularity. However, a large back-to-back private yard is still preferred by well over 50 percent of buyers, according to the NAHB poll, while 31 percent said they preferred a small back-to-back private yard, and 12 percent said they preferred a smaller yard with a common greenbelt.

The exterior. What is the house made of? A wood frame house will need repainting every 3 to 5 years. Siding can last 20 to 30 years or more, although it may eventually need painting, so check the age. A brick house saves the expenses of painting. According to various surveys, most people prefer brick, next stone, and last wood. The problem is that both brick and stones are very expensive, and thus most people settle for either a combination of brick and wood siding or aluminum or vinyl siding, and few stone houses are being built.

You'll need an expert to tell you about the structural soundness of the house. But instead of being dazzled by a home's curb appeal, you can eye a home from the outside as a curbstone critic to spot potential trouble spots. Here are some tip-offs excerpted from Freddie Mac's Consumer Home Inspection Kit.

An Exterior Checklist

EXTERIOR DRAINAGE

If properly located on its lot, drainage will be away from the home. Low areas around homes located on the low end of a fairly steep hill may collect water. A sump pump may be necessary to protect the home from moisture in the basement.

- Notice the areas around a home that have a high water table, sliding subsoil, underground springs, ledges or other similar problems. Surface grading should be highest next to the home so that water is carried away. If lot grading is correct, there should be no standing water in the yard 24 hours after it rains.
- Check for low spots around downspouts, standing water after it rains, signs of rot in wood, discoloration on brick or clogged downspouts. These are all signs that water is collecting next to the home and may be seeping into the basement.
- Notice whether patios, porches and driveways are slanting away from or toward the home. While it's relatively easy to regrade the ground, tearing out concrete and repouring it are expensive.
- Look at retaining walls, because their replacement cost is high. Check for cracks or signs of movement indicating poor construction or maintenance. If moisture is caught behind a retaining wall, it will freeze and expand, causing cracks in the wall.

EXTERIOR FINISHES (SIDING)

There are many different types of home siding, from traditional brick to vinyl, and often more than one type of siding exists on a home. Their looks and maintenance vary according to the type and condition of the materials. Aluminum siding, for example, looks similar to wood and the baked-on finish is almost maintenance free. Vinyl siding has replaced wood in newer homes.

Asbestos siding is made of the same materials as an asbestos roof. Its permanent finish does not need painting but will accept paint well. Anyone removing it should be extremely careful to avoid breathing in asbestos fibers. Removing and replacing asbestos siding should be done by a qualified, certified professional. When hiring a contractor to evaluate the situation, make sure the contractor has no connection with any remediation or abatement firm.

Stucco, on the other hand, is considered by some to be a high-quality finish.

- Check to see whether water is behind the wood in English Tudor half timber, half stucco homes.
- Check to determine whether the stucco is on masonry or frame. A hollow sound indicates frame. Stucco on frame is extremely susceptible to water penetration, particularly at the home's corners and around windows and doors. Water penetration is more likely if the cracks between the stucco and wood trim are not properly caulked.
- Check brick siding carefully because it may need to be repointed and repaired. While ivy-covered brick walls are attractive, English ivy will damage the home's mortar, especially in older homes. Grape ivy may be less harmful but should be kept away from wood trim because it can grow under the rim.
- Check to make sure that wood clapboard siding is painted and away from moisture problems. While it will last the life of the home if well maintained, wood clapboard siding should be carefully inspected for rotted boards. Pay particular attention

to any wood close to the ground, a likely area for rot and termites.

- Make sure that composition siding board is well maintained, painted, and away from moisture to prevent deterioration.

GARAGES

A garage is an important selling feature of a home, with a replacement value of over $7500 for a single-car garage and over $9000 for a double-car garage.

- Be sure there are a fireproof wall, ceiling, and door between an attached garage and the home. This should be ½-inch fire code drywall for the ceilings and walls or masonry and a solid core door.
- Make sure a two-car garage measures at least 20 × 20 feet and a single-car garage measures at least 14 × 20 feet. These measurements can be slightly smaller for compact cars.
- Remind the termite inspector to inspect the garage as well as the home for termites. Many old frame garages attract termites because the wood is resting almost directly on the ground.

GUTTERS AND DOWNSPOUTS

There are four major types of gutters: copper, aluminum, galvanized, and vinyl. Copper gutters, considered the highest quality, last almost a lifetime. Aluminum gutters, the most commonly used material for gutters, have a permanent baked-on finish. Galvanized gutters, used 30 to 40 years ago, have a normal life of 15 to 20 years, and must be painted regularly both inside and out. Vinyl gutters, used in recent construction, are relatively maintenance free except for cleaning.

- Check the condition and alignment of the home's gutters and downspouts.
- Make sure water is directed away from the home.
- Check to see if gutters and downspouts have pulled away from the home.

ROOFS

Asphalt or Fiberglass Shingle Roofs

In the last 30 years, asphalt or fiberglass shingle roofs have been installed on most homes in the United States. They are durable, attractive, relatively inexpensive, and designed to last 15 to 20 years.

- Check to see if an asphalt/fiberglass roof is aging. Evidence of aging includes exposed bare spots where the granules have worn away. You find this easy to see on a light-colored roof but more difficult to detect on a dark roof. If you're in doubt, try checking around the downspouts for granules collected at the outlets.
- If the shingles are pulling up at the ends, a condition known as "fish-mouthing," the roof is deteriorating. The slots between the shingles, or keys, are the weakest part of the roof and will wear out quickly.
- Be sure to check the south side of the roof and the area with the lowest pitch. Because sunlight is the major cause of deterioration, these areas will wear out fastest, even while the other side of the roof appears to be in good condition. In this case, a second asphalt/fiberglass shingle roof is normally installed directly over the first roof without removing the first layer of shingles. Before installing a third roof, both of these layers are removed down to the sheathing.

- Look at the edge of the roof to see how many layers exist. If there are three layers of shingles on a roof, the roof may be unable to carry the extra weight of another layer and the nails won't go all the way into the sheathing.
- Ask the seller whether the roof has been replaced recently. If a home is 18 years old with the original roofing intact, the roof will probably need replacing soon. On the other hand, if a home is 24 years old and has a second roof, that roof is probably only six to eight years old and will last for many more years.

Slate Roof

Slate roofs are considered to be deluxe roofs, usually good for the life of the home. There are many different grades of slate. Good Vermont slate, for example, can last 50 to 75 years without deteriorating, while Bangor slate may start to shale and deteriorate within 40 years.

- Check a slate roof carefully for signs of scaling or brown stains, which indicate deterioration. The roof may need frequent maintenance and replacement within a few years.
- If the home has a slate roof, ask the seller to replace missing slates and to tar the ridge before you buy the home.

Wood Shake and Cedar Shingle Roof

Wood shake and shingle roofs have experienced a revival in recent years. They cost about a third of the price of slate.

- Check to see if the roof is low pitched because machine cut cedar shingles will probably rot in about 12 years. However, heavy butt edge shakes on a steep pitch roof will last 15 to 20 years.

Be Your Own Appraiser

There are lots more details to check. To help you, Table 6-4 provides a checklist for items outside the house that was created especially for this book. It combines the standard appraisal form with our own tips.

Table 6-4 Checkpoints for Outside Evaluation of a House

Item	House 1	House 2	House 3
Address	___	___	___
Asking price	___	___	___
Type of home:			
Single-family	___	___	___
Semidetached	___	___	___
Condo	___	___	___
Town house	___	___	___
Age of home	___	___	___
Style	___	___	___
No. of stories	___	___	___
Location Features:			
Urban, suburban, rural	___	___	___
Built up (Over 75%, 25%, 75%, under 25%)	___	___	___
Growth rate (rapid, steady, slow)	___	___	___

(continued)

Table 6-4 (*Continued*)

Item	House 1	House 2	House 3
Property values (increasing, stable, declining)	_____	_____	_____
Demand/supply (shortage, in balance, oversupply)	_____	_____	_____
Present land use:			
(___% 1-family)	_____	_____	_____
(___% 2–4-family)	_____	_____	_____
(___% apartments)	_____	_____	_____
(___% condo)	_____	_____	_____
(___% commercial)	_____	_____	_____
(___% industrial)	_____	_____	_____
Change in present land use (not likely, taking place)	_____	_____	_____
Predominant occupancy (owner, tenant)	_____	_____	_____
Single-family prices $_____to $_____	_____	_____	_____
Predominant value: $_____	_____	_____	_____
Single-family age: _____to_____	_____	_____	_____
Predominant age: _____years	_____	_____	_____
Neighborhood Features (Rate 1–10)			
Employment stability	_____	_____	_____
Closeness to jobs	_____	_____	_____
Convenience to shops	_____	_____	_____
Convenience to school	_____	_____	_____
Quality of schools	_____	_____	_____
Public transportation	_____	_____	_____

Table 6-4 (*Continued*)

Item	House 1	House 2	House 3
Closeness to hospitals	____	____	____
Recreation facilities	____	____	____
Adequacy of utilities	____	____	____
Property compatibility	____	____	____
Police protection	____	____	____
Fire protection	____	____	____
Appearance of homes	____	____	____
Commuting	____	____	____
Privacy	____	____	____
Noise level	____	____	____
Lot Features			
Lot size	____	____	____
Corner lot (yes, no)	____	____	____
Slope of land:			
Away from house	____	____	____
Toward house	____	____	____
Drainage	____	____	____
Sidewalks	____	____	____
Storm sewer	____	____	____
Curb/gutter	____	____	____
Streetlights	____	____	____
Landscaping (1–10)	____	____	____
Garage (1–3-car)	____	____	____
Carport (covered?)	____	____	____
Driveway (straight, circular)	____	____	____
Utilities (aboveground, underground)	____	____	____

(continued)

Table 6-4 (*Continued*)

Item	House 1	House 2	House 3
Fenced yard	_____	_____	_____
Street location: (busy, not busy, dead end)	_____	_____	_____
Backyard (big, small, average)	_____	_____	_____
House Features			
Exterior walls:			
Brick, wood, siding, stone	_____	_____	_____
Roof material	_____	_____	_____
Age of roof	_____	_____	_____
Gutters/downspouts	_____	_____	_____
Storm windows	_____	_____	_____
Patio	_____	_____	_____
Swimming pool	_____	_____	_____
Deck (covered, not covered)	_____	_____	_____
Porch	_____	_____	_____
Screened porch	_____	_____	_____
Screens	_____	_____	_____
TV antenna	_____	_____	_____
Cable TV	_____	_____	_____
Tennis court	_____	_____	_____
Basketball court	_____	_____	_____
Trash collection (how often, cost)	_____	_____	_____
Security lighting	_____	_____	_____
Special assessments	_____	_____	_____
Other	_____	_____	_____
Overall Rating (1–10)	_____	_____	_____

CHAPTER 7

Shopping for a Good Buy—the Inside Story

What you want in a house comes first. But you also need to look at the inside of a house through the eyes of future buyers so that you can get the best investment for your money. Chances are that whatever will appeal to future buyers will also appeal to you.

Don't be deterred by cosmetic blemishes such as ugly wallpaper, worn carpeting, or out-of-date appliances. Envision what the house could be like with a little fixing up. That's what pays off in the end.

So where do you start?

See What's Cooking with the Kitchen

The salesperson may want to show you the spacious living room or the fancy dining room. The wise buyer knows that these are important, but that they aren't the rooms that count most. The first thing you should do is head for the kitchen. A large kitchen is the way to a home buyer's heart. Even though the American Restaurant Association reports that people are spending more

---

Mike's Favorite Home Improvement Story

In 1956 in Columbus, Ohio, after we had been in the United States for 4 years, we were ready to buy a house. The house we liked was appraised at $16,500. I offered $15,000, to which the seller said, "I can't do that."

"So fine, keep it," I said. In less than a day the seller was back. We bought the house. It was a mess, built in the 1930s. Immediately we began to improve it. We put in a new kitchen, two new bathrooms, and an unfinished lower level that had an exposed walk-out entry. Since I was in construction, building houses, the actual out-of-pocket expenses were nominal. It was mostly my "sweat equity," rebuilding the entire house.

A year and half later, we sold the house for a cool $23,000, a 53 percent improvement. That was some money at that time! The median price of new homes was $15,000, that of existing homes was $14,000, and median income was $5,200.

---

money eating out (three times as much compared to the pre-McDonald's 1930s), they still want a big kitchen. If they had their way, the kitchen in their dream house would be twice as big as the kitchen in their current house.

Look for an up-to-date kitchen with modern appliances, modern flooring, a dishwasher that works, chopping blocks, good outside ventilation, lots of cupboards, and a sizable pantry. A new kitchen offers a wide variety of innovations. One of these may be a butcher-block island, complete with a vegetable sink and an overhead pot rack with stained-glass inserts, placed in the center of the kitchen. Make sure the kitchen is big enough for a table and chairs.

According to consumer surveys, home buyers believe that a good kitchen must be bright, sunny, easy to clean, and close to the garage or carport for ease of bringing in groceries. Indeed, the design of the kitchen is important to buyers, according to surveys. Most consumers surveyed prefer more counter space, rather than an island counter space. They want a kitchen next to the family room. They also want a pantry and a bay window. (See Figure 7-1.)

One of these surveys provides clues explaining the interest in the kitchen. The survey asked people to rate the importance of different activities in the home, and 62.8 percent cited cooking and informal eating (see Table 7-1). And as everybody knows, the kitchen is where everybody gathers during a house party.

Figure 7-1   A Cozy Kitchen

Phot by James F. Wilson.
Source: Builder Magazine.

Table 7-1 Importance of Activities in the Home

Cooking and formal eating	62.8%
Reading	41.9
Watching TV	32.2
Socializing/informal entertaining	30.4
Listening to music	27.5
Hobby activities	19.6
Office-type desk work	19.2
Supervising children at play	18.1
Formal dining and entertaining	16.6
Family table games	8.3

Source: Michael Sumichrast and Gopal Ahluvalia. Copyright ©1985 by National Association of Home Builders, originally published in "Decisions for the 1990s."

Bolt for the Bathroom

Your next stop should be to check the bathrooms. The bathrooms, and how they are designed, are important to buyers. First of all, one is not enough. There should be at least two and a half and preferably three, including a private one in the master bedroom. An enclosed shower stall is better than a bathtub; Americans prefer showers to baths. And these days, a sauna or Jacuzzi is often an added attraction.

Bathrooms are important because they are highly visible to visitors and a place to show off the attractiveness of a home. They are also the utmost expression of privacy. The best ones are large enough to turn around in, with shiny new features. His-and-hers bathrooms (or at least sink basins) are in. An old-fashioned bathroom (with plain sinks instead of modern-looking basins and vanities, for instance) stands out like a sore thumb. And in housing, the rule of sore thumbs is that they turn off potential buyers. Unless you are prepared to spend $15,000 to $35,000 to update the bathrooms, stay away from homes with outdated bathrooms.

The trend in bathrooms is very clear. In 1972, when the U.S. Bureau of the Census began collecting data on new homes, 53 percent of the homes had two or more bathrooms. That had increased to more than 80 percent in 1990 and is now close to 100 percent. In the consumer surveys, practically no one indicated that one bathroom would be enough.

Barge into the Bedrooms

You shouldn't rest easy about a house until you see the bedrooms. You need at least three, and maybe four. As families became smaller, demand for a fourth bedroom eased somewhat in the early 1990s, but it began to increase again in 1996. The percentage of new homes with four or more bedrooms totaled 36 percent in 2002, compared with 23 percent in 1987 (see Table 7-2).

Even though people don't have as many children now, working couples often want an extra room for an office, computer room, or library. And, of course, these days each child expects to have his or her own room.

Look for bedrooms with privacy, privacy, privacy. Find a house with a master bedroom separated from the rest of the house by a Great Wall of China if you can, or at least by a hallway. This really sells. The other major demand for bedrooms is for closet space. There is never enough. When asked to choose their preference for a master bedroom from five basic layouts, consumers overwhelmingly picked the one with the walk-in closet.

Find the Family Room

Family rooms have traditionally been important to home buyers. They still are, but with the trend toward smaller families, an increasing number of consumers say a den would be sufficient.

A place where homeowners can get away and relax is important to most people and will be to future buyers. The family room is where many homeowners spend the bulk of their leisure time, watching television, reading, playing with kids, or just

Table 7-2 Characteristics of New Single-Family Homes

	1987	1992	1993	1994	1995	1996	1997	1998	1999	2000	2001	2002
Total completed (000)	1123	964	1039	1160	1065	1129	1116	1160	1270	1242	1256	1325
Central A.C. installed	71%	77%	78%	79%	80%	81%	82%	83%	84%	85%	86%	87%
2 1/2 baths or more	38%	47%	48%	49%	48%	49%	50%	52%	53%	54%	56%	55%
4 bedrooms or more	23%	29%	30%	30%	30%	31%	31%	33%	34%	35%	37%	36%
1 fireplace or more	62%	64%	63%	64%	63%	62%	61%	61%	61%	59%	58%	58%
Full or partial basement	39%	42%	40%	39%	39%	37%	37%	37%	36%	37%	35%	34%
Slab	43%	38%	40%	41%	42%	44%	45%	45%	47%	46%	48%	50%

No garage or carport	18%	15%	14%	13%	14%	13%	13%	12%	12%	11%	11%	10%
2-car garage or more	65%	75%	77%	78%	76%	78%	78%	79%	81%	82%	82%	82%
Brick exterior	18%	21%	21%	21%	20%	21%	21%	21%	21%	20%	20%	20%
1 story	49%	48%	48%	49%	49%	49%	49%	48%	48%	47%	46%	47%
2 stories or more	46%	47%	48%	47%	48%	47%	49%	50%	51%	52%	53%	52%
1200 sq. ft. or less	13%	10%	9%	9%	10%	9%	8%	7%	7%	6%	6%	5%
2400 sq. ft. or more	21%	29%	29%	28%	28%	30%	31%	32%	34%	35%	38%	37%

(continued)

Table 7-2 (Continued)

Average sq. ft.	1905	2095	2095	2100	2095	2120	2150	2190	2223	2266	2324	2320
Median sq. ft.	1755	1920	1945	1940	1920	1950	1975	2000	2028	2057	2103	2114
Median lot size, sq. ft.*	9295	9750	9680	9600	9508	9200	9000	8992	9071	8930	8927	8612
Average lot size, sq. ft.*	17,600	17,865	17,486	17,492	17,695	17,225	16,675	15,913	16,627	17,826	16,035	16,454

*Denotes number for new homes sold (beginning in 1992 condos are excluded). Not available for homes built on owner's lot.

Note: With the exception of total completed, average square feet, median square fee, median lot size, and average lot size, numbers are percentages.

Source: U.S. Census Bureau.

socializing. Make sure the house you are considering will be a comfortable place where you can relax.

Home buyers like the family room to be close to the kitchen. The consumer survey shows that most people prefer an arrangement in which the kitchen is visually open to the family room with a divider. Kitchen and family room areas that are side by side with a wall between them follow this. The next choice is two completely separate areas.

But the days when buyers must have a family room may be giving way to the day of the den. Given a choice and the right price, a growing percentage of consumers say that a den would be sufficient (see Table 7-3).

Table 7-3   A Den or a Family Room?

	1980	1985	1995	2003
Must have family room	50.0%	34.3%	30.0%	25%
Den is sufficient	50.0%	65.7%	70.0%	75%

Source: 2003 Consumer Preference Survey conducted by the National Association of Home Builders.

Through the House

Look closely at the rest of the house. Go back to where you started and look at the entrance. A foyer inside the front door has more appeal than a house where the door opens right into the living room. A good-looking door is an invitation to the house. There are so many beautiful types of front doors now available that it is a clear sign of neglect to be confronted with a plain, outdated 40- or 50-year-old entrance.

IS THE LIVING ROOM LIVABLE?

This is the showplace of the home, even if you don't use it much. Examine the layout and make sure that the room will fit the furniture you want to put in it. Don't end up with a living room with several short walls if you have a huge sofa. The picture window may be picturesque, but can you arrange your furniture around it? Do the carpeting and the wallpaper or paint suit your taste, or will you need to do extensive remodeling? What about the floor? Is there a hardwood, well-maintained floor? These days, wood floors are in, carpeting is out. But if the house does have carpeting, is it in good shape, or is wearing out? Is the main window looking at the street or at the back yard?

ENVISION DINING IN THE DINING ROOM

Check the size and make sure your dining room table will fit. How is the access to the kitchen? What is the chandelier like? Remember, a separate dining room has more appeal that a dining L off the living room. After dinner, do you have to schlep your guests back through the kitchen?

GO DOWN TO THE BASEMENT

Is it a finished basement, or will you have to remodel it someday? A basement that has been refinished as a separate bedroom or family room is more valuable that a traditional recreation area. Is it an exposed basement? Does the basement have an outside entry? If so, does it open directly to the yard, or do you have to climb stairs to get out? While you are down there, check the electric wiring and ask for an estimate of the electricity usage.

Changes in the design of new homes indicate what is in demand with buyers. What's in today includes many items that were considered luxuries several years ago. Builders today offer optional items such as gas fireplaces, kitchen and dining room pass-throughs, French doors, built-ins, room extensions, dormers, and finished recreation rooms on the lower level.

AMENITIES THAT NO LONGER ARE AMENITIES

There are other "must" items for a house if it is to be a good investment (see Table 7-4).

- Fireplaces are provided in more that 72 percent of all houses these days, up from 38 percent in 1972, because more buyers demand them. They do help sell houses, new or used.
- Central air conditioning no longer is a luxury. About 78 percent of all new homes have central air conditioning, up from 43 percent in 1972. The lack of central air conditioning will cool a buyer in the wrong way.
- Openness of design attracts buyers. People like to have a feeling of space when they walk into a house. That means that the old cubicle type of house with a bunch of small rooms is likely to turn off buyers, especially in these days of more move-up buyers. According to consumer surveys, floor layout is among the most important factors to buyers.
- Energy-efficient homes are important to home buyers. The energy crisis of the 1970s, although long forgotten, is still of concern, not only to drivers but especially to homeowners. It should be of concern to you, too. Check to make sure the house has modern storm windows, that its windows are properly caulked, and that it has storm doors that fit well. You're ahead if the furnace and air conditioning are newer, high-efficiency models that use less energy.

GREEN HOME TIPS

You can get more information on energy-efficient housing from mortgage giant Fannie Mae in its booklet, "Home Performance Power: Fannie Mae's Guide to Buying and Maintaining a Green Home." The booklet offers tips on maintaining a house at peak efficiency and offers tips on saving money on utilities and other energy-related bills. To get a free copy, call Fannie Mae toll-free during weekday business hours at (800) 732-6643.

Table 7-4 Consumer Preferences: New Homes
Costing $150,000 and $350,000

	$150,000 Home	**$350,000 Home**
Type/Area	S.F. detached Single story Preference: outlying suburb or close-in suburb	S.F. detached Two stories Preference: outlying suburb or close-in suburb
Size	1800 sq. ft.	3000 sq. ft.
Kitchen	Completely open or visually open	Completely open or visually open
Bedrooms	Three	Four or more
Bathrooms	Two or two and a half	Three or more
Washer/Dryer	Kitchen area or near bathroom	Near bedroom
Parking	2-car garage	3-car garage
Siding	Vinyl or brick	Brick, concrete, stucco, or wood
Products	Maybe brand name, but not necessary	Brand name products necessary
Windows	Vinyl window/ double pane	Wood window/ double pane
Skylight	Not necessary	Necessary
French door	Preferred, but not necessary	Necessary
Molding	—	Ceiling crown molding
Fireplace	Wood-burning	Wood-burning/Gas
Kitchen cabinets	Light wood	Light wood
Walk-in pantry	Must have	Must have
Microwave	Built-in	Built-in
Island work area	Must have	Must have
Extra-long counter in solid surface	Must have	Must have
Toilet, tub, and shower	White	White
Separate shower	Preferred	Preferred
Multiple showerhead	—	Preferred

Table 7-4 (*Continued*)

	$150,000 Home	**$350,000 Home**
Linen closet	Must have	Must have
Whirlpool tub	—	Must have
Exhaust fan	Must have	Must have
Ceramic tile walls/bathroom	Must have	Must have
Specialty areas	Laundry room Dining room Sun room	Laundry room Dining room Sun room Media room Home office
Soundproofing	Preferred	Preferred
Front porch	Preferred	Preferred
Deck/patio	Preferred	Preferred
Exterior light	Preferred	Preferred
Ceiling height	8 ft.	9 ft. or higher
Amenities	—	Whole-house wiring Multiple phone lines Multizone HVAC
Complex	Park area Playground Walking/jogging trails	Park area Playground Walking/jogging trails Open space for community
Flooring: Entry Foyer	Ceramic/hardwood	Ceramic/hardwood
Flooring: kitchen	Vinyl	Hardwood or ceramic tile
Flooring: bedroom	Carpet	Carpet/hardwood
Flooring: bathroom	Ceramic/vinyl	Ceramic
Flooring: hallway	Carpet	Carpet/hardwood
Security system	—	Must have
Central vacuum system	—	Must have

Source: "What 21st Century Buyers Want," Copyright ©2001 by National Association of Home Builders.

Still More Costs to Consider

You have to consider the cost of living in the house you buy. There are several costs that you should check.

UTILITY BILLS

Find out how the house is heated and cooled. Natural gas was the cheapest for heating, but costs have been trending up. Oil is second. Electric heat generally is still the most expensive. Heat pumps, which are also used for cooling, can hold down the costs in all-electric homes.

Make sure you see the utility bills for an entire year. Check the heating bills in the dead of winter. What are the air-conditioning costs at the height of summer? Also check the water bills. You can ask the local utility company to estimate typical bills for the house you are considering.

To help cut costs for homeowners, the Department of Energy is working with mortgage lenders to roll improvements into standard mortgage packages. A list of lenders offering energy-efficient mortgages is available from the Energy Department, the FHA, the VA, and Fannie Mae.

PROPERTY TAXES

Find out how much the annual property taxes are. Divide by 12 to see what will be added to your monthly payments. The real estate agent showing the home usually provides this information. Ask to see receipts for the past several years. This tells you how fast taxes are rising. Also find out if the house has been reassessed upward since the last tax payment. You can call the tax collector's office in the area in which you are looking for a home to get tax information.

ASSESSMENTS

See if there are any special assessments that you will have to pay. For example, if you must join a community association, find out how much the fees are. This will automatically be part of the cost for most condominiums to help pay for the common areas, like a swimming pool, tennis courts, and other facilities. Many single-family developments also have community associations, so don't forget to check on this even if you aren't going condo.

APPLIANCES

Check the appliances throughout the house. How old are the washer and dryer? Do the washer and dryer come with the house? How aged is the refrigerator? How soon will such appliances need to be replaced, and at what cost? Use our wear-out checklist to see. Then you can negotiate a lower price or seek replacement of the appliances by the owner before you move in.

STRUCTURAL CHECKPOINTS

Another major attraction of any house is the quality of construction. Consumers are very quality-conscious and attach great importance to quality features in a home. Buyers can spot certain quality features, such as hardwood floors or finely crafted trim. But few of us are expert enough to spot serious structural flaws or other basic problems. That is why you should never buy a house without making the sale contingent on a professional home inspection.

> *Test the plumbing.* Turn on the bathroom sink faucet and the shower, then flush the toilet. When the toilet starts to refill, does the water pressure diminish markedly? Fill sinks and bathtubs with 3 inches of water. Do they drain properly? Do faucets leak? Lift up any carpeting. Are there signs of flooding or decay?
>
> *Look over the interior.* Is the plaster badly cracked? Are walls and ceilings straight and level? A newly painted interior may look nice, but it could be hiding something. Do door and windows open easily? Are there signs of leaks?

Look for evidence of termites in basement wood structures. Is there wood or paper debris? Do you see termite tubes or tunnels? Termites travel to and from the earth, so make sure there are no places where the earth is closer than 6 inches to wood.

MORE SIGNS TO WATCH FOR

Check the basement for water. Look for dampness on the walls or signs of water seepage into the floor drain. Move away any objects obscuring the view of the basement walls. Many times they are put there to cover the signs of mildew or water. Inspect a house right after a heavy rain. Sometimes wetness is a result of poor gutter alignments or bad gutters. Water can be detected by discoloration of floor tile, stained paneling at floor level, and dark spots on cinderblocks.

Check the electric wiring. Many older homes aren't wired for today's electric living, with hair dryers, TVs, videocassette recorders, stereos, and you name it. A house should have at least 100 amps and preferably 200 amps. The number of amps is usually listed on the service panel of the fuse box or circuit-beaker box. When you look there, you should see something that indicates whether you have an extra-heavy 220-volt outlet for heavy appliances, such as a washer and dryer.

Check the outlets. Check for grounded three-prong outlets, especially if you plan to plug in a computer or power tools. Also count the outlets in each room. Newer homes have outlets every 12 feet to avoid the need for extension cords.

Smoke detectors. Make sure the house you buy has at least two smoke detectors that sound an alarm in case of a fire. Most areas now require smoke detectors in any house sold. If your house doesn't have them, they are inexpensive to install.

Radon. Another problem in some areas of the country is an odorless, colorless radioactive gas called radon that can cause lung cancer. The gas can be detected only by using special monitoring equipment. If a house has radon, getting rid of it can cost a few thousand dollars. A check for radon should be part of the home inspection if the gas has been detected in homes in your area.

Copper pipe—pinhole leaks. Homes built before 1970 are exposed to what water specialists call "pinhole leaks." These leaks can cause extensive water damage and can be very expensive to fix. They occur in cold-water, horizontal copper pipes. In just two counties in Maryland, Montgomery and Prince George's, there are approximately 21,000 miles of copper pipes running in homes. The counties are experimenting with the injection of orthophosphates into the water filtration process, a practice commonly used to reduce pipe corrosion. Nationally, about 50 percent of water treatment facilities use some type of phosphate to control corrosion. The cost of this treatment is going to be passed on to homeowners.

Note: In old areas, there is the continual problem of replacing the leaking old cast iron pipes that deliver water with cement, mortar-lined, ductile iron pipes. This is also a costly and disruptive problem found in just about all older neighborhoods.

Get an Inspection

Here are some other items to check on the inside, according to Freddie Mac. The full checklist is available at www.freddiemac.com.

Walls and Ceilings

In nearly all homes built before World War II, the walls and ceilings were made of plaster. While the exterior walls in a brick home built before 1935 are usually built with the plaster directly on masonry, the walls are very solid, though they don't provide for air space or prevent condensation.

The interior walls and ceilings in a home built before 1935 are usually made of plaster on wood lath. Over time, wood lath loses its resilience and pulls away from the studs or joists, causing waves in the walls or ceilings.

- Check to see if wallpaper over wood lath and plaster has been painted. If you try to remove the painted wallpaper, you may damage the plaster.
- Check for walls and ceilings that are made of rock lath and plaster, which is common in homes built between 1935 and 1950. Typically, these are very high quality.
- Check the condition of drywall walls and ceilings. Pay particular attention to the condition of taped joints.

Windows

As you conduct your home inspection, be aware of the many different types of windows in the home and their condition. Steel casement windows, for example, are not generally considered to be quality windows because they become sprung, readily conduct cold air into the home and will only take piggyback type storm windows. Replacement hardware is available but is becoming increasingly expensive. Steel casement windows can easily be replaced with new, double hung vinyl replacement windows.

Wood double hung windows are very common, especially in older homes. They're likely to be in good condition, and storm windows will usually make them more energy-efficient.

Aluminum sliding windows, which were often installed in the 1950s, are inexpensive but serviceable. They are now available with insulated glass, but storm windows are usually less expensive.

Jalousie windows do not provide adequate insulation and leak air at a tremendous rate.

- Open the windows to ensure that they are not painted shut.
- Check the casement window to see if the hardware is working properly and whether double hung.

Floors

If the floors are carpeted, check to see if the carpeting covers hardwood or plywood floors. In newer homes, plywood is typically used. Hardwood floors are better and usually considered to be a distinguishing feature.

- Check the condition of the floors or carpet. Ask the seller to replace the carpet or other floor covering or to refinish wood floors if necessary.
- Check for moisture damage to parquet floors. In older homes, the parquet is made of strips of wood glued into nine-inch square blocks. This flooring is extremely sensitive to moisture and can swell and buckle when exposed to dampness. A newer type of parquet flooring is made of one-half-inch or three-quarter-inch plywood with a hardwood and laminated finish. This flooring is much less sensitive to moisture and can be safely installed even below grade at the basement level.
- Determine if the house has asbestos floor tiles. The asbestos in the tiles is "cementitious"; that means the asbestos fibers are bound in place within the tiles and probably cannot become airborne, potentially breathable and therefore a health hazard. If you choose to have asbestos-containing tiles removed, be sure the work is done by qualified, certified professionals.

Insulation

As fuel costs continue to rise, insulation is an increasingly important consideration in a home. It's usually difficult to tell whether insulation exists within the walls of a home. As a rule, if the home has little or no attic insulation, there is probably none in the walls. If the attic is well insulated, the walls probably will be too, depending on the age of the home.

Basements

It is important to inspect the basement carefully. All the major mechanical, plumbing and heating systems in a home are usually located in the basement. It is also the only part of a home where exposed piping, wiring and framing can almost always be seen. Foundation or structural problems may also be detected in the basement, and they typically affect the entire home.

- Check the basement walls for large cracks or any noticeable defects. Also look for signs of movement, particularly in an older home. Hairline vertical cracks along the mortar joints and concrete block are not usually causes for alarm. A crack that indicates a serious problem will be at least 1/4-inch wide all the way through to the outside wall. In some cases, horizontal cracks that are 1/2-inch wide or wider, and have caused the wall to bow out, stem from pressure building up behind the wall from the outside. In order to correct the problem, this pressure must be relieved. Be sure to have your professional inspector check this.

  If the cracks are very wide and there's been significant settlement, the footings or foundation were probably poured on fill ground. In this situation, it might be necessary to underpin. Your professional home inspector will be able to determine the extent of and solution to the damage. Be aware that settlement cracks in a basement floor slab are not usually structurally significant, but they may indicate either the compacting of fill dirt on which the slab was poured or the presence of an underground spring.
- Examine the condition of the mortar between the bricks or cinder block when you look at the basement walls. In many older homes, the original mortar will have deteriorated

and need pointing up in order for the wall to maintain structural integrity.

- Check all the wood structural members in the basement for signs of rot or termite damage. In most parts of the country, termites are subterranean and will almost always be found where the wood is close to the ground.
- Pay particular attention to the sill plate around the perimeter of the exterior walls (the 2 × 6 or 2 × 8 that is bolted to the top of the masonry foundation walls). Termites can also enter where there is concrete on the exterior, for example, under a concrete porch or around a fireplace hearth.
- Look for signs of work done since the home was built. If additional support columns were installed, for example, it's important to determine why it was done. It might mean the home has a structural defect.
- Inspect the deterioration of materials and other factors that might affect the livability of the home. For example, if the basement is not at least 7-$\frac{1}{2}$ feet high, it will probably not be usable as living space. While some codes permit a basement recreation room or bedroom to be as low as 6$\frac{1}{2}$ feet high, 7$\frac{1}{2}$ feet is considered the minimum for living standards.
- Be aware of unfaced stairs, deteriorated stair treads, leaky doors, and windows that are frozen open or shut.
- Check for the presence of asbestos. This can only be verified by an expert, but can be spotted in heat pipe coverings in older homes, packing material on old hot water and steam boilers and fireproof materials in furnace rooms. If your professional home inspector finds it, you may wish to leave it in place, if it is in good condition, not friable and not likely to deteriorate. Or you may want to negotiate the cost of having it removed or encapsulated.

Hot Water Heaters

- Check the age and size of hot water heaters to see if they've been recently replaced or are of greater than average capacity (see Table 7-5).

Table 7-5 Hot Water Heater

Number of Occupants	Gallons Recommended
2	30 gallons
5	40 gallons
6 and over	50 gallons

Be Your Own Appraiser—Compare Houses

Even before you buy, you can do some close inspection yourself to compare homes. Table 7-6 provides a buyer's checklist for items inside the home.

Table 7-6 A Checklist for Inside the House

	House A	House B	House C
Address of house	____	____	____
City	____	____	____
Asking price	____	____	____
Homeowner's association fees	____	____	____
Square feet living area	____	____	____
Cost per square foot	____	____	____
Number of rooms	____	____	____
Number of stories	____	____	____
Number of bedrooms	____	____	____
Number of bathrooms	____	____	____
Attic (yes, no)	____	____	____
Construction (Rate 1–10, 10 highest)			
Quality of construction	____	____	____
Conditions of improvements	____	____	____

Table 7-6 (*Continued*)

	House A	House B	House C
Room size and layouts	___	___	___
Closets and storage	___	___	___
Insulation adequacy	___	___	___
Plumbing	___	___	___
Electric	___	___	___
Kitchen cabinets	___	___	___
Overall livability	___	___	___
Appeal and marketability	___	___	___
Other Items			
Floors (hardwood, carpet, other)	___	___	___
Walls (drywall, plaster, other)	___	___	___
Trim finish	___	___	___
Bath floors (ceramic, carpet, other)	___	___	___
Kitchen Equipment			
Refrigerator (cubic feet, age)	___	___	___
Range/oven	___	___	___
Disposal (age)	___	___	___
Dishwasher (age)	___	___	___
Fan/hood	___	___	___
Compactor (age)	___	___	___
Microwave (age)	___	___	___
Flooring (type)	___	___	___
Basement			
Finished/unfinished	___	___	___
Outside entrance	___	___	___

(continued)

Table 7-6 (*Continued*)

	House A	House B	House C
Concrete floor	_____	_____	_____
% Finished	_____	_____	_____
Carpeting	_____	_____	_____
Floor drain	_____	_____	_____
Sump pump	_____	_____	_____
Finished ceiling	_____	_____	_____
Finished walls	_____	_____	_____
Finished floors (carpet/wood)	_____	_____	_____
Evidence of dampness	_____	_____	_____
Features			
Fireplace	_____	_____	_____
Storm doors	_____	_____	_____
Storm windows	_____	_____	_____
Electrical service (in amps)	_____	_____	_____
Fuse box or circuit breakers	_____	_____	_____
Hot water heater (gallons, age)	_____	_____	_____
Closet space	_____	_____	_____
Central air conditioning (age)	_____	_____	_____
Heating (gas, electric, oil; age)	_____	_____	_____
Furnace (size, age)	_____	_____	_____
Washer (size, age)	_____	_____	_____
Dryer (size, age)	_____	_____	_____
Heat pump (age)	_____	_____	_____
Ceiling fans (which rooms)	_____	_____	_____
Smoke detector (how many)	_____	_____	_____
Three-prong outlets	_____	_____	_____
Outlets per room	_____	_____	_____

Table 7-6 (*Continued*)

	House A	House B	House C
Sauna			
Jacuzzi			
Other Expenses			
Real estate taxes			
Gas bill			
Electric bill			
Water bill			
Cable TV bill			
Overall Evaluation			
Room to Room			
Level			
Foyer			
Living room			
Dining room (separate?)			
Kitchen			
Family room			
Master bedroom			
Second bedroom			
Third bedroom			
Fourth bedroom			
First bathroom (shower, tub)			
Second bathroom (shower, tub)			
Third bathroom (shower, tub)			
Kitchen (table space?)			
Basement (finished, unfinished)			

(continued)

Table 7-6 (*Continued*)

	House A	House B	House C
Family room	_____	_____	_____
Den	_____	_____	_____
Recreation room	_____	_____	_____
Attic (finished, unfinished)	_____	_____	_____
Overall rating (1–10)	_____	_____	_____

CHAPTER 8

A Home Isn't Always a House— Condominiums and Town Houses

The hot housing type of the twenty-first century just may be condominiums and town houses. They appeal to two key markets. First-time home buyers can still find condos for under $100,000 in many areas of the country. At the same time, more and more older people are buying upscale town houses after the kids leave home. As an added attraction for both groups, such homes usually are in communities that offer amenities such as swimming pools, tennis courts, and even golf courses.

In the past, condos and town houses weren't great investments because they didn't appreciate in price as much as single-family houses. But this is changing, too. In 2000 the median sales price of a condo or town house was nearly 20 percent lower than the median price of a single-family house. By 2003, the gap had narrowed to 3 percent.

What is a condominium, anyway? Actually, *condominium* is a legal term for a type of shared ownership rather than a type of housing. In fact, condos come in all shapes, sizes, and prices.

- *High-rise condominium apartments*. These are apartments in buildings of more than three stories. Some are 20 stories high or more.

- *Low-rise, or garden, condominiums.* These are apartments in buildings up to three stories high. They typically have a garden type setting, with walks, gardens, and outdoor recreational facilities.
- *Town houses.* These are row houses connected by common walls. Town houses are more like houses than like apartments; many have an upstairs and a basement.
- *Cooperatives or co-ops.* These are buildings in which apartment owners buy shares in the entire building.

There also are self-sufficient condos that are not part of any housing development (see Figure 8-1).

Figure 8-1   Town House Living

Photo By Anthony Traub.
Source: Builder Magazine.

How Does a Condo Compare with a House?

The living space in an average condominium is a few hundred square feet smaller than that in an average single-family home (see Table 8-1). But some condos and town houses are as big as or bigger than most single-family houses.

THE RISE, FALL, AND REBIRTH OF CONDOS

The condo concept isn't new. The first written documents for such housing date to before the Roman Empire. Legend has it that even Julius Caesar went out one day and bought a condo unit; in the sales office, he ran into an old friend who was buying. And Caesar said to him, "Et tu, Brute?"

Okay, so we made up that last part. But the rest is true. The condo concept was around during the rise and fall of the Roman Empire and was widely used in Europe for centuries. It still is. The main reason is the shortage of land.

Table 8-1   Selected Features of New Single-Family and Condominium Homes

	1980		1990		2002	
	Singles	**Condos**	**Singles**	**Condos**	**Singles**	**Condos**
Average lot size (SF)	11,600	2,377	10,043	2,395	12,000	2,350
Average living area (SF)	1,658	1,237	1,762	1,325	1,900	1,400
Number of bedrooms	3.5	2.0	3.8	2.2	4.1	2.5
Number of bathrooms	2.8	2.0	3.0	2.3	3.5	2.5

Source: National Association of Home Builders unpublished report.

In the United States, condos came in with a bang in the early 1970s. They started in California (where else?) and swept east, becoming especially popular in Florida and New York. Between 1970 and 1972, the number of condominiums in the United States increased 15-fold to nearly 1.3 million units. After the condo craze came a condo crash. By 1974, many areas were overbuilt. Prices of condos, especially in resort areas, fell sharply.

Then came the condo comeback, as condominiums became an established part of housing. Today more than 14 million people live in more than 6 million condominium units. Condo living is here to stay.

Spurred by low interest rates, condominiums and town houses sold at a record clip in 2003, with sales rising to 896,000

Mike's Favorite Condo Story

In 1972, my friend Carl Freeman began to build high-rise condominiums in Bethany Beach, Maryland. He made us a deal we could not refuse: a one-bedroom one-and-a-half-bath, 725-square-foot condo unit for $32,500, or $44.80 a square foot. With equity from the sale of our beach house near there, we bought the condo unit. We had a beautiful view of the Atlantic Ocean, and we loved it—that is, we loved it until our three boys became teenagers. The project was called Sea Colony, and our boys started to call it Dead Colony.

So we sold it after 15 years, and we doubled our money. A similar 725-square-foot unit was being offered in January 2004 for $415,000, or $572 a square foot. In 1991, my wife, Eva, and I bought a small unit in Prague, in the Czech Republic, where Eva comes from. We paid less than $5000. Prague is thousands of miles away from being called "dead." So we have kept that condo.

existing units from 706,200 (see Table 8-2). It was the eighth straight year of record sales. In addition, new units were built in 2003, up from 35,900 in 2000.

The comeback has been so strong that condos have become an increasingly good investment. Indeed, between 2000 and 2003, the median price of existing condos and town houses went up 39 percent, to $163,800, compared with a 25 percent jump in the median price of single-family homes, to $170,000 (see Table 8-3).

Table 8-2 Sales of Existing Condo Apartments and Co-ops, 1995–2004

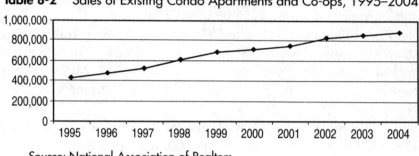

Source: National Association of Realtors.

Table 8-3 Existing Condo Apartments and Co-Ops, Units Sold and Median Sales Price

Year	Units Sold	Median Sales Price
1990	348,000	$85,200
1995	428,000	87,400
1996	476,000	90,900
1997	524,000	95,500
1998	607,000	100,600
1999	681,000	108,000
2000	706,000	111,800
2001	746,000	123,200
2002	820,000	142,500
2003	898,000	163,800
2004e	970,000	182,000

e = authors' estimate.
Source: National Association of Realtors.

A major advantage of condominiums is that they can be built more cheaply than single-family houses because they have 25 percent less space on average and occupy considerably less land.

Yet many of the condos and town houses being built today are very expensive, as builders are catering to the more affluent. Many units are built on costly ground in the downtowns of cities or on the waterfront. Some are as big and as fancy as single-family houses. As a result, the median price of new condominiums has soared to $200,000 from $139,000 in 2000.

Still, a snapshot of condo construction shows that nearly a third are priced below $150,000 (see Table 8-4).

Prices also vary by region. The cheapest condo units are in the South, where the median price is around $136,100, compared with a median of $204,800 in the West region. Midwest and Southeast condos are priced at about $176,700 and $163,500, respectively. (See Table 8-5.)

We think condos and town houses will continue to appreciate. For one thing, a lot of younger people are buying condos. The big demand will be in the middle to upper prices as the giant baby boom generation ages and moves to their preretirement or retirement housing. They will be looking for homes with lower

Table 8-4 Condominium and Co-Op Units for the
12 Months Ending Third Quarter 2003

Asking Price	Units Completed	%
Under $125,000	7,800	18.7
$125,000–$149,999	4,800	11.4
$150,000–$199,999	7,500	18.0
$200,000–$249,999	3,700	8.9
$250,000–$299,999	3,300	7.9
$300,000 or more	14,600	35.1
Median asking price	$210,200	100.0%

Source: U.S. Census Bureau, Survey of Market Absorption.

Table 8-5   Median Sales Price of Existing Condos and Co-Ops

Year	U.S.	Southeast	Midwest	South	West
2000	$111,800	$111,200	$121,700	$ 87,700	$136,800
2001	$123,200	$124,200	$134,900	$ 97,100	$141,900
2002	$142,200	$147,000	$148,600	$114,500	$171,600
2003	$163,800	$176,700	$163,500	$130,600	$204,800
2000–2003	+46.5%	58.9%	34.3%	48.9%	49.7%

Source: National Association of Realtors.

upkeep and less maintenance. For many, that will be a condo or town house rather than a big single-family house.

Even at higher interest rates, condominiums and town houses "remain very attractive and coincide with a strong underlying demand for housing," said David Lereah, chief economist for the National Association of Realtors.

Is Condo Living for You?

You should shop for a condo just as you would for a house, looking for appealing units in growing areas. Individual town houses often appreciate more rapidly than units tied to ownership of common elements.

So if you want to go condo, go ahead—just shop around carefully. And before you take the plunge, ask yourself the following question: Is condo living for me?

This is no idle question. The condominium way of life isn't for everybody. In a condo project, your neighbor is as close as the other side of your wall. And keeping the project running smoothly requires the cooperation of all the residents. So think hard: What is your lifestyle? Do you prefer to be left alone or to mix with other people? Do you mind following rules?

A study by the Department of Housing and Urban Development noted: "Some of the most widespread problems in multifamily ownership structures are the problems of communal living. Both traditional renters, who have had the landlord as an arbitrator of disagreements, and traditional single-family home owners, who are often unprepared for high-density living, have significant adjustments to make in a multifamily ownership situation."

In a multifamily development, your condo may be your castle, but you aren't always king of it. Condo developments are run by rules set by the majority of owners through the community owners' association or by the elected board members. That means that if you want to paint your outside door blue and the association says it must be white, you have to paint the door white. There also usually are restrictions on such things as TV antennas, certain types of remodeling, and sometimes even children and pets.

You share in the ownership of the land, together with the rest of the owners, and the part of the building in which your unit is located.

"Condominium living sometimes means bowing to the will of the majority as determined by the elected board of directors who run the project," said one Chicago property management official. "But this can be trouble if the board decides, for example, to raise your assessment fee to pay for new tennis courts and you don't play tennis."

Such differences can lead to "internal strife," as the HUD study called it. Whether pets should be allowed can often cause

---

Mike's Favorite Dog Story

After we sold our house in Columbus, Ohio, and moved to Washington in 1963, we moved into an apartment at 5000 Townsend Way, Bladensburg, Maryland. After the first week, my wife, Marika, was called to the manager's office. "We were told that you have a dog in your apartment. Is that true?"

"Of course it's true. So what?" asked my wife.

"This is one of the buildings we do not allow pets in," said the manager. "We have to move you into another building."

"No, you won't. I would rather move out of this project," Marika said.

And so we did. We bought a very good brick three-bedroom, two-bath, two-story house with a finished basement in Bethesda, Maryland. It cost $27,000. And we could take our dog with us.

Moral: If you have a dog (or two, as we now do), make sure pets are welcomed before you buy into a project.

---

a major conflict. It is, the HUD study said, "largely a conflict between the dog lovers and the dog haters of the world."

This certainly was a major problem in the past, and it still continues to some extent, but more and more projects today are offering "pet friendly" apartments and condominium units.

Don't let anybody discourage you. Despite all the rules, many condo owners are quite happy with their choices. In fact, many are happy *because* of the rules. And don't forget that many new single-family housing developments with common recreational facilities and owners' associations have similar rules.

"These communities also provide some degree of protection against neighborhood degradation and deterioration—cars on cinder blocks, dilapidated homes, yards that are not maintained or even the infamous flock of pink flamingos," says the Community Association Institute, an association of community associations.

Condo Shopping: What to Look For

If you are ready to "go condo," there are certain things you need to check.

LOCATION

Where the condo is located is the prime concern, just as for a detached house. Find a condo in a growing neighborhood, especially one in which there is demand by the type of buyers who lean toward multifamily living. Follow the advice in this book on shopping for a house; but with condos, you will have some special features to consider.

CONSTRUCTION

Poor construction can be a major problem with any home, but it can be a nightmare in a condominium building. You will share walls with your neighbors, and inadequate soundproofing can be a major problem. This was the most frequently mentioned problem identified in the HUD study. Thin walls remain a common complaint, so find out if your future walls have ears. When you are looking at a development, have someone go next door and stamp around so that you can hear how much of the noise comes through to your side. If someone lives there, you can even ask him or her to turn the stereo or TV on full blast so that you can hear how much of the sound penetrates. Most people would not mind at all.

You don't want to smell somebody else's cooking while you're eating or taking a walk in the hallways.

As with any home, make your purchase contingent on a satisfactory inspection of the soundness of the structure. Then make sure that the inspector knows something about condos, including the areas of the project where you share ownership with others.

COMMON AREAS

With a condo purchase, inspecting the soundness of your unit isn't enough. You will share responsibility for all common elements of the project, from the shared roof to the swimming pool. If these common structures have a big defect, you may have to pay to fix them.

Make sure the owners' association at the project you buy into has reserves sufficient to cover one-time expenses.

CONDO FEES

You will be charged a monthly fee to cover the upkeep of the development, including its management, as well as the cost of recreational facilities. This can range from $100 to several hundred dollars a month that you pay to the condo association in addition to your monthly mortgage payment to your lender. So make sure you can afford all the payments. The assessments aren't voluntary. You need to think of them as part of your mortgage payment.

What You Need to Know

Here is some basic advice from the Community Association Institute, an association of community associations (www.caionline.org):

When you have your eyes on a particular home, the first thing you should do is ask the real estate agent if it's part of a community association. If so, obtain copies of the governing documents, including the Covenants, Conditions & Restrictions (CC&Rs), from the association manager or a volunteer community leader. Read this information carefully. If you don't understand something, ask your agent or attorney for guidance.

It is essential that prospective buyers remember that homeowners—explicitly or implicitly—agree to comply with CC&Rs when they move into an association-governed community. These rules and regulations apply to assessments, procedures, architectural guidelines (such as additions, decks and paint colors), maintenance, satellite dishes, clotheslines, fences, animals, patios, landscaping and more.

You can also talk to people who live in the community. Find out how they feel, not only about the neighborhood, but also about how the community is governed and managed. Take a walk. Are the common grounds well maintained? Are the homes well kept? Is there ample parking? Are the amenities—swimming pools, tennis courts and playgrounds, for example—well maintained? Ask to talk to a volunteer community leader—the president of the association, a member of the elected board or the professional who manages the community.

At a minimum, you should be able to answer the following questions before you buy a home in a community association:

- How much are the assessments, and when are payments due?

- What do the assessments cover?
- What is not covered and, thus, what are your individual responsibilities as a homeowner?
- What is the annual budget?
- Does the community have a viable reserve fund?
- Are there restrictions on renting property?
- Do the architectural guidelines suit your preferences?
- Is the community age-restricted? If so, what is the policy on underage residents?
- Are there simmering issues between homeowners and the elected board?
- What are the rules with respect to pets, flags, outside antennas, satellite dishes, clotheslines, fences, patios, parking, and home businesses?

ASSESSMENTS: YOU GET WHAT YOU PAY FOR

Before buying a home in an association-governed community, you should examine the association budget carefully because it sets the level of assessments and services. Collected monthly, quarterly or annually, assessments are not voluntary. They are mandatory homeowner dues that must be paid or the association can take legal action, such as placing a lien against your property, an action that can lead to foreclosure. More importantly, as a member of that community, it is your obligation to pay your fair share of the costs.

Determine what the assessment covers and what it does not cover. Assessments typically cover expenses for items such as maintenance of common areas, trash collection, snow removal, private streets, recreational facilities, and other amenities. In some communities, assessments cover exterior maintenance to units. For those who live in homeowner or condominium associations, assessments rarely cover monthly mortgage payments, real estate taxes, or interior maintenance. However, principal, interest, and real estate taxes are often covered in the monthly fee for cooperatives.

Determine if the budget includes a reserve fund for major expenditures. Virtually all communities will require large expenditures at some time—roofs replaced or private roads and parking areas resurfaced, for example. If a reserve fund is not part of the budget, the association will likely have to impose a special assessment when major projects become necessary—and that can be an expensive and unanticipated financial burden.

SPECIAL ISSUES AND CIRCUMSTANCES

- *Newly developed communities:* Determine not only when but also how the developer plans to transition control of the community to homeowners.
- *Resale:* Consult a community association manager or association officer to determine if there are unresolved issues pertaining to that property, delinquent assessments and unapproved architectural changes, for example.
- *Buying to rent:* Examine the CC&Rs with respect to regulations affecting rentals. And remember, it will be your responsibility to educate your renters and ensure they abide by the association's rules and regulations.

BE REALISTIC—UTOPIA DOESN'T EXIST

You've identified your ideal home. You've done your homework. You're ready to buy. But there's one more thing on your checklist: Resolve to manage your own expectations. Like any endeavor involving people, community association living is not utopia. With all their inherent advantages—and there are many—community associations can face difficult issues, many of them connected to the need to balance the rights and responsibilities of individual homeowners with those of the community as a whole. Community associations are not unlike any human enterprise. Judgments are subjective and subject to change. Decisions are not always met with unanimous approval. Mistakes are made. Human beings—residents and community leaders—may occasionally lose sight of what's right, fair, and reasonable.

As you ponder your own expectations, remember that some personalities are not suited for community association living. Some people bristle when faced with rules and regulations that must be enforced to maintain established community standards. Ask yourself if you're likely to have severe buyer's remorse the first time you run up against a rule you don't like. If you're not sure, think it over. Talk to people who live in the community.

Finally, don't overlook the most important questions: Is it the right kind of community for you and your family? Does it fit your lifestyle and sense of community? Does it provide the amenities you want—a community pool, recreational opportunities, attractive common grounds, ample parking, and proximity to schools? Is it a good investment?

The basic documents to check include the following:

THE CONDOMINIUM SALES CONTRACT

This is the first document you will be asked to sign. The agreement should completely describe your unit, the purchase price, and the method of paying. It should also state how much the monthly assessment is. Don't sign it unless you are satisfied that you know as much as you want to about the property you are buying.

THE MASTER DEED

This is sometimes called the declaration. This is the controlling condominium document. It should fully describe the size, location, and mechanical equipment in each condominium home. For your protection, look for definitions and a detailed description of these additional items: the scope of the project itself, the owners' association, common elements, the purposes for which the building and each of the units may be used, provisions for assessments and charges, and management agency documents.

THE BYLAWS

The bylaws are the provisions for administering and maintaining the condominium complex. They will greatly affect what you can and cannot do with your unit and could affect your ability to resell it in the future.

In studying the bylaws, you should check several important points. What are the rules and regulations governing the owners' association? What are the duties and powers of the owners or their elected board of directors? If the project is new, make sure that the developer doesn't have too much power. The point at which the developer will turn over the control of a new project to the owners should be clearly defined. If you are buying in an older project, check with other owners to see how well the owner's association manages the property.

PROTECT YOUR RESALE RIGHTS

Check the covenants and restrictions regarding resale. Can you sell your unit to anybody you want, or do you have to offer it first to the condominium association? This is called a "right of first refusal." Similarly, the association may have the right to clear prospective buyers before you sell your unit to them. Some argue that this helps to maintain the value of the homes, but it may also limit your ability to sell your condo. Avoid any development with such rules.

Remember, you and your fellow owners are in charge of running your housing complex. When you buy a condo, you are, in effect, becoming a member of a mini-government.

The homeowners' association goes through several phases after a new project is built, according to one HUD report. The first is the *honeymoon period,* when the developer is still running most of the operation. The point at which the developer leaves and turns the operation over to the owners is sometimes called the *awakening period,* the report said.

"At this point, owners come to realize that they are the HOA (homeowners' association). Original owners begin moving for a variety of reasons. The owners of specific units become increasingly more difficult to keep current as the units are sold to new owners without HOA notification. Dues collections began to falter. Replacement reserves and methods for calculating and predicting costs are found to be inadequate. Latent construction defects surface, but the builder's one-year warranty has expired. Subcontractors cannot be located . . . inadequately designed community facility equipment begins to fail, particularly swimming pools and irrigation systems. Monthly fees are found to be inadequate to meet current expenses. HOA directors feel isolated, frustrated and resign, drop out or refuse to run for additional terms. Residents begin to violate architectural, parking and pet restrictions. HOA finds enforcement power unspecified."

Most owners' associations, however, overcome their growing pains and move into what the report called the *coming of age period.* In an existing development, many owners are old pros at running the association smoothly. With a little checking, you can find out if your prospective owner's association has come of age or if it is still in for a rude awakening.

More Condo Questions

The late Marika Sumichrast, who was in charge of a large condo project at Leisure World in Silver Spring, Maryland, always advised, "Don't buy from paper and ask plenty of questions." She had a list of condo questions that she would ask, most of which apply to both new and resale units. The list is still good today. It goes like this:

- Can you afford it? Can you afford to carry the mortgage, including property taxes, and the association fee? What is the fee? Who controls it, the developer or an owners' association? In estimating expenses, add 10 to 20 percent to what you read in the brochure to be safe.
- Is the sales price comparable to the prices of other available housing? The cost per square foot should be about the same as for similar housing.
- Can you resell the unit and get appreciation comparable to that with other housing? How have the homes appreciated in value over the years? How are they selling now?
- Will your heat and dollars go up the chimney? Is the home you are about to buy energy-efficient? Insist on knowing the insulation R-value, the types of windows and doors, and the cost of utilities.
- Find out who has to fix what. That's something you can't get away from. Find out what your maintenance responsibilities are and what the owners' association will take care of.
- Check the builder's reputation. Find out from other people living there, the homeowners' association, or resale agents such things as, has he ever built a condo development before? Has he ever built anything before? What's his record? Is he solvent? What do financial people think of him?
- Does the developer take care of warranty work? What is his reputation for taking care of complaints promptly and fairly?
- Is the developer running the management, or is the management of the community independent from the developer? If management is independent, find out its reputation for running the community and responding to residents' requests and complaints.
- What is the quality of the project? What do people who live in the community think about their homes? Are they satisfied,

or do they complain about inferior work? Are individual buyers or the community suing the developer for unfinished or inferior work?

- What is the durability of the housing and common facilities?
- Will there have to be a lot of renovation in the next 2 or 3 years? What is the life expectancy of roofs, carpets, appliances, elevators, heating and air-conditioning equipment, and other items?
- What kind of security does the community provide? Is it real or only on paper?
- Insist on inspecting your home at least 14 days before settlement. Make a list of needed work. Go back again before settlement to see whether the work was done. Never go to settlement without all items having been taken care of to your satisfaction.
- What are the restrictions on what you can do with your home?
- Don't believe what they tell you about costs. Chances are it will cost more. Make sure you have some idea how much more.

CHAPTER 9

Negotiating the Best Deal

In the animal imagery of Wall Street, investors are divided into bulls and bears. Similar creatures are involved when people are negotiating for a house. Bulls are ready to charge into a deal quickly, even though there are red flags that should make them wary. Bears are more cautious, often letting the negatives outweigh the potential. But when it comes to negotiating a deal for a house, the best animal to be is a fox. Do your homework ahead of time so that you can make wise negotiating decisions based on the situation.

A home is too big a purchase to make a hasty decision about. Tough negotiating doesn't mean that you're a great talker or an aggressive deal maker. Mainly, it means learning as much as you can about the transaction so that you can get the best deal.

What Kind of Market Are You In?

How you bargain for a house depends to a large extent on market conditions. Basically, there are three types of housing markets.

Seller's market. In a seller's market, the supply of housing is short and demand is strong. In this market, you will probably have to bid near or at the asking price in order to get the house you want. In some cases, buyers may even bid more than the asking price. A seller's market is characterized by low interest rates and rapid increases in prices. Sellers' markets were often seen during the record low interest rates in 2002 and 2003.

Buyer's market. In a buyer's market, the supply of housing for sale far exceeds the number of shoppers. That's when price discounting is heavy. This is the time to make a ridiculous offer on a house that you otherwise can't afford, bargain hard to get a better price on the house you want, or get the seller to help pay some of your closing costs.

Normal market. Frequently, the number of houses for sale and the number of home hunters are fairly well balanced. To get the best buy, you have to be a sharp shopper. That's where learning to be a fox comes in.

Your best bet is to find out as much as you can about the housing market and the seller so that you can negotiate from strength.

When you go house hunting, the late Washington, D.C., veteran developer Frank Calcara suggested, you should keep in mind three golden rules:

Rule 1: Don't fall in love with a house and lose your senses. You don't marry a house. It is an investment.

Rule 2: Buy only what makes economic sense to you.

Rule 3: Have a basic idea of what you want and what you are willing to pay. Then stick to it!

Sharpen Your Negotiating Skills

Know the prices of similar houses in the area. That way you will know a good price when you hear one. Thanks to the Internet, these days it is easy to find out exactly what other houses in a neighborhood have sold for.

Look at at least a half dozen houses so that you know first-hand what the market is and how the house you are considering compares.

Find out how long the house has been on the market. If it's been several months, the buyer is probably getting anxious and will be more willing to lower the price.

Find out about the sellers. Are there reasons they might be eager to make a deal? Maybe they have already purchased another house and need money from the one they are selling. Or maybe they have been transferred to another city and need to sell.

Revisit a house that appeals to you, but this time go with a strictly negative point of view. You know the positive points. This time, look for things that might cause problems. If you see things that don't satisfy you, you can bargain to have the seller fix them or reduce the price to cover the costs of your doing so.

MAKE YOURSELF A DESIRABLE BUYER

Sometimes you can get a house even if you don't make the best offer. The seller may prefer to sell to someone who seems certain to complete the deal as soon as possible rather than someone who, despite a higher bid, may run into problems. Make it clear that you're a serious shopper.

How do you do this?

Try not to need the contingency that you must sell your house first. If you already own a home, try to sell it before you go house hunting. If you don't own a home, you are already ahead of those who must sell. A seller prefers to have what is in effect a cash deal rather than take the risk that a buyer might scrap a deal if her own house fails to sell.

Be prepared to show that you are financially able to buy a house. One way is to get prequalified for a mortgage. This will show sellers that you're not an underfinanced fledgling who would love to buy a house but doesn't know if he can afford it.

Don't make impossible demands. One New Jersey house hunter had difficulty finding a house because of one inflexible demand: The basement had to be at least 40 feet by 23 ½ feet. The man was building his own airplane and needed that much space to work on it. Demanding hard-to-find features will probably cost you more.

What if somebody else gets a contract first on the house you want? Get a backup contract. If someone puts a contract on a house, that doesn't necessarily mean that the person will buy it. If you agree on a backup contract, you are next in line if the first deal falls through. And since you know that the seller has already lost a buyer, you know that he or she may be willing to negotiate new details.

Ask about a "kick-out clause." If a seller has just accepted a contract on a house that you want, ask if the sale was contingent on the buyer's selling his or her own home. Some contracts contain a clause stating that if a seller gets another contract without a home-sale contingency, the first buyer has 48 hours to sign a new contract without the contingency or the house can be sold to the second buyer.

Making the Offer

Usually you don't do face-to-face bargaining with the seller. You negotiate through the real estate agent, who is out to sell the house for her or his client—which isn't you. That means that you are negotiating with a professional. The good ones always smile, smile, smile. They don't run to greet you. As a great professional at selling, Jim Mills, advised salespeople, "Don't swoop on them." The good ones are always ahead of you. They know their product. "If you knew the market like I do, you'd know what a great buy this is," they will say.

We don't mean to imply that you can't trust the salesperson who is trying to sell you the house. We just want you to remember that the final decision must be yours. Keep your negotiating strategy to yourself. If you make an offer in a contract, the agent or

Realtor is obligated to present that offer to the seller, no matter how low the offer may be. (Not all agents are Realtors, by the way. A Realtor, with a capital R, refers to a member of the National Association of Realtors. Realtors subscribe to a code of ethics.)

Often, the real estate agent acts as a necessary buffer between the emotions of the seller and those of the buyer. That's what Mike Sumichrast's late wife, Marika, discovered.

Mike's Favorite Negotiating Story

When Marika Sumichrast was a real estate agent, she used to say: " If I let them [the buyer and the seller] talk directly to each other, they may cut their throats. So I have to bounce back and forth. Sometimes I think [negotiators] have an easier job talking to the Israelis and Arabs than I have talking to buyers and sellers."

Bidding on a house can be tricky. If you bid too low, you may get rejected. But you don't want to pay too much. What should your strategy be?

As we mentioned, this is based on your evaluation of the market. In a fairly normal market, one strategy is the "halfway" approach. Determine how much below the asking price you think is reasonable, then make an offer that is twice as much below the asking price. If the seller offers to meet you halfway, you will get your price. For example, if a house is on the market for $200,000 and you want to pay a maximum of $190,000, make an offer of $180,000. If the seller splits the difference, you will pay $190,000.

Once you know the market, the best strategy sometimes is to bid the "comp." That is, find the comparable prices that similar homes have sold for and bid that amount less 5 or 10 percent for "wiggle room." The real estate agent will also know the comparables and will see that your offer is in the ballpark when she or he presents it to the seller.

Another strategy is to make an offer that is close to the asking price but ask for concessions. If you will be paying mortgage points, ask the buyer to split the cost with you. If repairs to the house are needed, ask the seller to share the expenses. Still other strategies are given in Table 9-1.

Restrain your bullheaded instincts. Bargain hard, but not on a take-it-or-leave-it basis. Don't turn down a deal over a few thousand dollars. Stretched over a 30-year loan, the difference may be peanuts for the house you want.

Writing the Contract

When you are ready to make an offer on a house, you don't just ask the seller what he or she will take. You must put your offer in writing. The seller will usually come back with a counteroffer. Then you can get down to business. Any promises by the seller must also be in writing. Oral promises aren't worth the paper they aren't written on.

Legal contracts can be intimidating, so you should familiarize yourself ahead of time with the contracts used in your area. A typical contract is given as Table 9-2.

A sales contract binds you to certain legal obligations. You should know what each line in the contract means. The following are key points that you should look for in a contract. And remember, no matter what is printed on a contract before you sign it, the first law of home buying is: "Everything is negotiable."

WHAT TO LOOK FOR IN A CONTRACT

1. *The date of the contract.* It is important that the date be correct because contingency provisions in the contract are based on the date. So don't forget to check the date.
2. *Your name.* Even this isn't as simple as it may seem. Don't say in the contract that you, Mr. and Mrs. Jones, are the buyers unless you are absolutely sure that this will be the case. For instance, you may change your mind before the settlement,

Table 9-1   Bidding Strategies

Here Is a Summary of More Bidding Strategies: Technique	When Most Effective	Possible Outcomes
Start low and move up	Works best for properties that are overpriced in slow markets	Seller rejects outright or counters to get you to increase your offer, and you move up and agree on a price that comes close to what you want to pay
Offer close to asking price	Works best for properties that are priced well in active markets	Seller may accept outright or counter to get you to increase offer slightly
Offer the top price you can afford	Works best in hot markets	Seller may reject, and you may have to walk away
Save terms to bargain	Works best in situations where seller is highly motivated	Seller may trade price concessions for your agreement to close sooner or take charge of repairs after the inspection
Give up something to get something	Works in most situations	Seller ends up taking something you don't really want, but ask for initially to gain a lower price or other concession
Move in small increments	Works best for overpriced properties in slow markets	Seller may agree to lower price if given time to adjust to the idea
Focus on issues you can resolve to keep momentum going	Works best after several rounds of negotiation	Seller and buyer come to terms after resolving easiest issues first
Be unpredictable	Works best after several rounds of negotiation	Seller accepts your offer after you suddenly make a sizable change
Make an either/ or offer	Works best after several rounds of negotiation	Seller accepts one of two scenarios you offer
Split the difference	Works best after several rounds of negotiation	Seller and buyer settle on price exactly between asking price and offer
Set deadlines for action	Works best in any situation	Seller and buyer will act more quickly and decisively if given a time limit

Source: Inman News Features.

Table 9-2 Residential Sales Contract

[R] REALTOR®

RESIDENTIAL REAL ESTATE CONTRACT (PAGE 1 OF 4)

[Equal Housing Opportunity]

1. **1. THE PARTIES:** Buyer and Seller are hereinafter referred to as the "Parties."

2. Buyer(s)_____ Seller(s)_____
3. _____(Please Print)_____ _____(Please Print)_____
4. **2. THE REAL ESTATE:** Real Estate shall be defined to include the real estate and all improvements thereon. Seller agrees to convey to Buyer or to Buyer's designated
5. grantee, the Real Estate with the approximate lot size or acreage of _____

6. commonly known as: _____
7. _____Address_____ _____City_____ _____State_____ _____Zip_____
8. _____
9. _____County_____ _____Unit # (if applicable)_____ _____Permanent Index Number(s) of Real Estate_____
10. **3. FIXTURES AND PERSONAL PROPERTY:** All of the fixtures and personal property stated herein are owned by Seller and to Seller's knowledge are in operating
11. condition on the Date of Acceptance, unless otherwise stated herein. Seller agrees to transfer to Buyer all fixtures, all heating, electrical and plumbing systems together with the
12. following items of personal property by Bill of Sale: [Check or enumerate applicable items]

12	__ Refrigerator	__ All Tacked Down Carpeting	__ Fireplace Screen(s)/Door(s)/Grate(s)	__ Central Air Conditioning
13	__ Oven/Range/Stove	__ All Window Treatments & Hardware	__ Fireplace Gas Logs	__ Electronic or Media Air Filter
14	__ Microwave	__ Built-in or Attached Shelving	__ Existing Storms & Screens	__ Central Humidifier
15	__ Dishwasher	__ Smoke Detector(s)	__ Security System(s)	__ Sump Pump(s)
16	__ Garbage Disposal	__ Ceiling Fan(s)	__ Intercom System	__ Water Softener (owned)
17	__ Trash Compactor	__ TV Antenna System	__ Central Vac & Equipment	__ Outdoor Shed
18	__ Washer	__ Window Air Conditioner(s)	__ Electronic Garage Door Opener(s)	__ Attached Gas Grill
19	__ Dryer	__ All Planted Vegetation	with ____ Transmitter(s)	__ Light fixtures, as they exist
20	__ Satellite dish and system	__ Invisible fence system	__ Home Warranty $____	

21. **Other Items included:** _____
22. **Items NOT included:** _____
23. Seller warrants to Buyer that all fixtures, systems and personal property included in this Contract shall be in operating condition at possession, except:_____
24. _____. A system or item shall be deemed to be in operating
25. condition if it performs the function for which it is intended, regardless of age, and does not constitute a threat to health or safety.
26. **4. PURCHASE PRICE:** Purchase price of $_____ shall be paid as follows:
27. Initial earnest money of $_____ by (check), (cash), or (note due on _____) to be increased to a total of
28. $_____ by _____. The earnest money and the original of this Contract shall be held by the Listing Company, as
29. "Escrowee", in trust for the mutual benefit of the Parties. The balance of the Purchase Price, as adjusted by prorations, shall be paid at closing by wire transfer of funds, or
30. certified, cashier's, mortgage lender's or title company's check (provided that the title company's check is guaranteed by a licensed title insurance company).
31. **6. ACCEPTANCE:** Earnest money shall be returned and this offer shall be void if not accepted on or before _____
32. **6. MORTGAGE CONTINGENCY:** This Contract is contingent upon Buyer obtaining an unconditional written mortgage commitment (except for matters of title and survey
33. or matters totally within Buyer's control) on or before _____ for a _____ (type) loan of
34. $_____ or such lesser amount as Buyer elects to take, plus private mortgage insurance (PMI), if required. The interest rate (initial
35. rate, if applicable) shall not exceed ____% per annum, amortized over not less than _____ years. Buyer shall pay loan origination fee and/or discount points not
36. to exceed ____% of the loan amount. Seller shall pay loan origination fee and/or discount points not to exceed ____% of the loan amount. Those fees/points committed
37. to by Buyer shall be applied first. Buyer shall pay the cost of application, usual and customary processing fees and closing costs charged by lender. (IF FHA/VA, refer to
38. Paragraph #38 for additional provisions.) Buyer [check one] □ will □ will not lock in the interest rate at the time of loan application. Buyer shall make written loan
39. application within seven (7) calendar days after the Date of Acceptance. **FAILURE TO DO SO SHALL CONSTITUTE AN ACT OF DEFAULT UNDER THIS CON-**
40. **TRACT.** If Buyer, having applied for the loan specified above, is unable to obtain a loan commitment and serves written notice to Seller within the time specified, this Contract
41. shall be null and void and earnest money refunded to Buyer upon written direction of the Parties to Escrowee. **IF WRITTEN NOTICE IS NOT SERVED WITHIN THE**
42. **TIME SPECIFIED, BUYER SHALL BE DEEMED TO HAVE WAIVED THIS CONTINGENCY AND THIS CONTRACT SHALL REMAIN IN FULL FORCE**
43. **AND EFFECT. UNLESS OTHERWISE PROVIDED HEREIN, THIS CONTRACT SHALL NOT BE CONTINGENT UPON THE SALE AND/OR CLOSING OF**
44. **BUYER'S EXISTING REAL ESTATE. A CONDITION IN THE MORTGAGE COMMITMENT REQUIRING SALE AND/OR CLOSING OF EXISTING REAL**
45. **ESTATE SHALL NOT RENDER THE MORTGAGE COMMITMENT CONDITIONAL FOR THE PURPOSE OF THIS PARAGRAPH. IF SELLER AT SELLER'S**
46. **OPTION AND EXPENSE, WITHIN THIRTY (30) DAYS AFTER BUYER'S NOTICE, PROCURES FOR BUYER SUCH COMMMITMENT OR NOTIFIES**
47. **BUYER THAT SELLER WILL ACCEPT A PURCHASE MONEY MORTGAGE UPON THE SAME TERMS, THE CONTRACT SHALL REMAIN IN FULL**
48. **FORCE AND EFFECT. IN SUCH EVENT, SELLER SHALL NOTIFY BUYER WITHIN FIVE (5) BUSINESS DAYS AFTER BUYER'S NOTICE OF SELLER'S**
49. **ELECTION TO PROVIDE OR OBTAIN SUCH FINANCING, AND BUYER SHALL FURNISH TO SELLER OR LENDER ALL REQUESTED INFORMATION**
50. **AND SHALL SIGN ALL PAPERS NECESSARY TO OBTAIN THE MORTGAGE COMMITMENT AND TO CLOSE THE LOAN.**
51. **7. CLOSING:** Closing or escrow payout shall be on _____, or at such time as mutually agreed upon, by the Parties, in writing. This sale
52. shall be closed at the title company escrow office situated geographically nearest the Real Estate, or as shall be agreed mutually by the Parties.
53. **8. POSSESSION:** Possession shall be deemed to have been delivered when Seller has vacated premises and delivered keys to premises to Buyer or to Listing Office.
54. Seller shall deliver possession to Buyer [check only one]:
55. □ (a) at the time of closing; **OR**
56. **[Do not complete the following option (b) unless possession is not to be delivered at closing.]**
57. □ (b) by 11:59 P.M. on _____, provided sale has been closed. In the event possession is not to be delivered at closing, Seller agrees to pay
58. at closing the sum of $_____ per day to Buyer for use and occupancy from and including the day after closing to and including the possession date
59. specified above, regardless of whether possession is delivered prior to the possession date. (See Paragraph #18)
60. **9. RESIDENTIAL REAL ESTATE AND LEAD-BASED PAINT DISCLOSURES:** If applicable, prior to signing this Contract, Buyer [check one] □ has □ has not
61. received a completed Illinois Residential Real Property Disclosure Report; [check one] □ has □ has not received the EPA Pamphlet, "Protect Your Family From Lead in Your
62. Home"; [check one] □ has □ has not received a Lead-Based Paint Disclosure.
63. **10. PRORATIONS:** Proratable items shall include, without limitation, rents and deposits (if any) from tenants, utilities, water and sewer, homeowner's or condominium
64. association fees. Seller represents that as of the Date of Acceptance Homeowner Association/Condominium fees are $_____ per _____. Seller
65. agrees to pay prior to or at closing any special assessments (governmental or association) confirmed prior to Date of Acceptance. The general Real Estate taxes shall be
66. prorated as of the date of closing based on ____% of the most recent ascertainable full year tax bill. All prorations shall be final as of closing, except as
67. provided in paragraph 19.
68. **11. OTHER PROVISIONS:** This Contract is subject to the GENERAL CONDITIONS and those OPTIONAL PROVISIONS selected for use and initialed by the Parties
69. which are contained on the succeeding pages and the following attachments, if any: _____

71. **THIS DOCUMENT WILL BECOME A LEGALLY BINDING CONTRACT WHEN SIGNED BY ALL PARTIES AND DELIVERED**

72. Date of Offer		DATE OF ACCEPTANCE
73. Buyer Signature	Social Security No.	Seller Signature	Social Security No.
74. Buyer Signature	Social Security No.	Seller Signature	Social Security No.
75. Print Buyer(s) Name(s)		Print Seller(s) Name(s)
76. Address		Address
77. City	State	Zip	City	State	Zip
78. Phone Number(s)	Email	Phone Number(s)	Email
	FOR INFORMATION ONLY	
79. Selling Office	MLS #	Listing Office	MLS #
80. Selling Agent	MLS #	Email	Listing Agent	MLS #	Email
81. Address, City, ST, Zip		Address, City, ST, Zip
82. Phone No.	Fax No.	Phone No.	Fax No.
83. Buyer's Attorney	Email	Seller's Attorney	Email
84. Address		Address
85. Phone No.	Fax No.	Phone No.	Fax No.
86. Mortgage Company		Loan Officer	Phone No.

- Page 1 of 4

and you may want to add a daughter or a son to the contract. Instead of spelling out the names, just insert "as purchaser may direct."

3. *Deposit.* On this line you agree to put down a deposit of a certain amount on the house. This is also known as earnest money. There is no legal requirement concerning this amount, but about 5 percent is generally acceptable. You should require that the funds be held by a neutral party in an interest-bearing account and that the interest go to you if the sale occurs.

4. *Price of the house.* This is where you write in what you are offering for the house. Make sure that it is correct because you are legally binding yourself to that price. During the bargaining, the price may change as you negotiate. You don't have to write a new contract every time; both you and the seller merely initial any changes. Give the seller a specific period of time, usually 5 to 7 days, to accept or reject the proposed contract.

5. *Financing.* In this section you state what kind of financing you expect to obtain (how big a mortgage and for how long), for example, "a $180,000 conventional mortgage for 30 years at a 6.5 percent annual interest rate." This is an estimate; the actual terms will depend on the mortgage you obtain. The sale usually is contingent on your obtaining a mortgage, and your contract should have a provision that if you cannot get the financing, your contract will be null and void, and you will get your deposit back. However, the contract usually requires you to seek financing within a specified period, such as 14 or 45 days, and you must make a bona fide effort to obtain financing or you could lose your deposit or be sued.

6. *Sale contingency.* If you have to sell your house first, you should include a clause saying that the sale is contingent on that.

7. *Loan fees.* When you obtain a mortgage, the lender will probably charge you a certain number of points for making the loan. Each point is equal to 1 percent of the loan amount.

When you sign a contract, you can negotiate to have the seller pay some of the points. Often the buyer and seller agree to split the points, up to a certain amount. But this must be written into the contract. You also should negotiate to have the seller pay part or even all of the closing costs, such as transfer taxes.

8. *Settlement.* The contract will specify a date when you will go to closing on the house. This is negotiable and should give you enough time to arrange financing and prepare to move. As the contract should note, you, as the buyer, have the right to select the title company, attorney, or other concern that will handle the settlement.

9. *Additional provisions.* If there are other contingencies to the purchase, they are included in an addendum. These are items that you want to make the sale contingent on, such as specifying that the washer and dryer are conveyed with the house.

10. *House inspection.* You definitely should make the sale contingent on an inspection of the house's structure. The clause should read something like this: "This contract is contingent upon the purchaser having the right to engage a professional inspector to determine the structure and conditions of the house. The inspection shall be conducted and the contingency removed within five working days from the date of the acceptance of this contract, and the inspection report must be satisfactory to purchaser or all deposit monies will be immediately refunded and all contract obligations shall be null and void."

11. *Provision for a walk-through.* The right to have a walk-through inspection of a house to make sure you are getting what you paid for or that agreed-upon repairs have been made should be in writing.

12. *Radon inspection.* In areas where the gas radon has been detected, you should include a provision in a home purchase contract specifying that the house is free of the gas.

13. *Termite inspection clause.* In this line, the seller agrees to have the house inspected for termites and to repair any

damage that might be discovered. This seems simple enough, but Benny Kass, a Washington, D.C., real estate lawyer and columnist, suggests some safeguards:

First, change the word *house* to read *property*. Second, watch out for such language as "based on a careful visual inspection." This often will not include basements, crawl spaces, or other inaccessible areas that, unfortunately, carry the greatest risk of termite inspection. Third, insist that the termite company provide you with a warranty for at least 1 year.

14. *The fine print.* Most home sales contracts are loaded with fine print that obligates you to all kind of things. You should read the small print carefully and object to anything you disagree with. Even the fine print can be negotiated.

Do You Need a Lawyer?

With such a major and complicated transaction as buying a house, the question of whether you should hire an attorney to look after your interests arises. This is not an easy question to answer, as the majority of home real estate transactions are closed without the benefits of an attorney. This is mainly because lawyers are quite expensive. In addition, most home transactions are not that complex, as deeds and contracts are fairly uniform. In addition, real estate brokers and title companies now offer some of the same services as lawyers.

Still, the decision to retain an attorney depends on the complexity of the transaction and the buyer's need for peace of mind. And the cost of hiring an attorney may be a small price to pay for that.

Buyer's Rights

These days, Realtors may "read you your rights" before you buy a house. These are mainly disclosures about a home and the agent's responsibilities. They usually include the following:

- You have the right to have a lawyer review your sales contract and to represent you. All contracts should be in writing, and an agent is required to submit all written offers to the seller.
- You have the right to select the lender, subject to negotiations with the seller over who should pay how many points.
- You should understand that the real estate agents, while they may aid you in purchasing a house, are agents of the seller. Agents should answer your questions honestly and should disclose material facts that they know about the property.
- You have the right, prior to signing a contract, to review the applicable master plan for the area in which the house is located.
- You have the right to make a purchase conditional on an acceptable report by a home inspection company hired at your expense.
- You have the right to equal treatment without regard to race, color, religion, national origin, sex, age, marital status, sexual orientation, presence of children, or handicap.

The Ultimate Weapon

Remember, in all this bargaining, you have a trump card. In the end, if the seller doesn't meet the price you are willing to pay, you don't have to buy the house. Even though you may think you will never find another house like this one, you will if you have to. If the seller knows you aren't bluffing, you will probably get your way. But if you don't, you must have the strength to walk away.

Don't do what the coauthor of this book, Ron Shafer, once did when he bought a house many years ago. He and his late wife, Barbara, weren't even looking for a house one summer day when he took their two children and a friend's two children to see a movie while the friend looked for a house. When Ron and the kids came out of the movie, his wife and her friend drove them to a split-level home in McLean, Virginia, that, it turned out, his wife wanted to buy. They bought it that very day—and soon ended up with three mortgages when they ran into problems selling their previous home: They had one mortgage on the old house, a short-term mortgage to pay the down payment on the new house, and the mortgage on the new home.

Meanwhile, in the light of day, Ron quickly realized that there were dozens of homes in the same neighborhood exactly like the one he had bought. Fortunately, the house turned out to be a great investment, but the Shafers could have saved money by not rushing into the deal. The movie Ron took the kids to see that day, by the way, was *Dumbo*.

CHAPTER 10

How to Mortgage Your Future and Find Happiness

Home loans have come a long way since the 1920s. Back then, you usually had to make a 50 percent down payment on a house and then finance the rest of the cost over only 5 years. The 5-year loan had a big balloon payment at the end, and if you couldn't pay off the loan at that time or get a new one, you lost your home. During the Great Depression of the 1930s, millions of people lost their homes when they couldn't pay their mortgages.

Today, you can get a mortgage for 30 years. Instead of a 50 percent down payment, you can put down as little as 5 percent or, in some cases, nothing. You pay back the money in monthly installments. In addition, there are a lot of new ideas in home financing, with everything from adjustable rates to the "two-step" mortgage.

Our ideas about mortgage rates have changed over the years. As late as the 1960s, the idea of a mortgage rate above 6 percent was shocking. A *New Yorker* cartoon by Al Kaufman showed a couple leaving a house with the wife angrily telling her husband, *"You might have told them my age after bragging that we have a 5¹/₄ percent mortgage on our house."*

During the recession of 1979 to 1981, we had to revise the first edition of *The Complete Book of Home Buying* to raise the mortgage interest tables to as high as 18 percent. These record-high mortgage rates decimated the real estate industry, as Mike Sumichrast experienced firsthand.

Mike's Not-So-Favorite Mortgage Story

During the last year of Jimmy Carter's presidency in 1980 and into Ronald Reagan's first term in 1981, the prime rate shot up to 21.5 percent. I was paying prime plus 1½ percent, or 22.5 percent, on a real estate investment of $2 million, and the record high rates were killing me. The high rates were also killing five million other people in construction and real estate. Even the best builders were falling like dominoes. Some of them just turned the keys of their homes over to the lenders. Who could pay 23 percent interest and survive? And who would be foolish enough to buy a home at an 18 percent mortgage rate? Not many people.

By 2000, mortgage rates had nosedived to the lowest rates in 40 years, 4 percent or less, setting off a stampede of home buying. Rates can't stay that low forever. The point to remember is that mortgage rates of 6 to 8 percent would be considered low by recent historical standards.

Where to Get a Mortgage

In the old days, when you went shopping for a mortgage, you were mainly limited to the local building and loan associations. Today you can borrow from everybody from your neighborhood bank or thrift to Internet lenders including E*Trade and Quicken to Mr. Goodwrench and General Motors Corporation's GMAC Financial Services.

Today commercial banks are aggressively competing with other institutions to lend mortgage money. With the blurring of laws governing the services banks can offer, many banks these days are calling themselves "financial services companies." Indeed, the nation's biggest mortgage lender is Wells Fargo Bank (or financial services company). Savings and loans, or thrifts, are still prime lenders. You can get loans from mortgage bankers. You can enlist mortgage brokers to find the best loan for you. Or you can search web sites yourself to get lenders to compete for your business. You can even apply for loans online. You also may be able to get a loan from a credit union where you work.

A look at a list of America's biggest mortgage lenders underscores the variety of lender options you have today (see Table 10-1).

Wherever you get your loan, it is likely to end up in the portfolio of one of three institutions: Fannie Mae, Freddie Mac, or Ginnie Mae. None of these outfits makes loans itself, but Fannie and Freddie are the biggest investors in residential mortgages in the United States. Together, they own or guarantee about 42

Table 10-1   Major U.S. Mortgage Lenders

ABN Amro Mortgage, www.mortgage.com
Bank of America, www.bankofamerica.com
Bank One, www.bankone.com
Branch Banking & Trust, www.bbandt.com
Cendant Mortgage, www.cendantmortgage.com
Countrywide Financial Corp., www.my.countrywide.com
Chase Home Finance, www.chase.com
CitiMortgage Inc., www.citibank.com
GMAC Financial Services, www.gmacfs.com
National City Mortgage, www.nationalcitymortgage.com
Sun Trust, www.suntrust.com
U.S. Bank, www.usbank.com
Washington Mutual, www.wamu.com.
Wells Fargo Home Mortgage, www.wellsfargo.com

percent of the $7 trillion U.S. mortgage market. Both companies package mortgages and sell mortgage-backed securities all over the world. Their government sister is Ginnie Mae, which is part of the U.S. Department of Housing and Urban Development.

Both Fannie Mae and Freddie Mac are private companies, but both are also government-sponsored. Critics say that this backing gives the companies an unfair advantage over their competitors. All three mortgage organizations are important to home buyers because they were created to provide a steady flow of mortgage money and to help keep mortgage rates down. They also have a huge impact on the types of mortgages that you can get.

What Kind of Mortgage Should You Get?

Today there are literally hundreds of different mortgages. Trying to pick the right one can be like trying to choose from all the flavors at your local ice cream parlor. But don't get confused. Despite all the choices, there are only two basic types of mortgages: conventional loans and nonconventional loans. And they come in only two flavors: fixed-rate mortgages and adjustable-rate mortgages. Everything else is simply a variation on those themes.

CONVENTIONAL MORTGAGES

Conventional mortgages are simply mortgages that aren't backed by the federal, state, or local government. The majority of buyers get this type of loan. The loans generally require a down payment of 20 to 25 percent of the purchase price and can run as long as 30 years. There are two types, conforming and nonconforming. Conforming loans are mortgages of up to $323,700. Nonconforming loans, also known as jumbo loans, start at $323,701 and generally have a slightly higher mortgage rate.

NONCONVENTIONAL MORTGAGES

These are loans that are backed by government agencies. The two major types are FHA loans and VA loans.

FHA Mortgages   These mortgages are backed by the Federal Housing Administration, which is part of the U.S. Department of Housing and Urban Development. The FHA doesn't make loans itself; it insures loans made by private lenders. Since this reduces the risk for lenders, the terms for FHA loans are somewhat more lenient than those for conventional loans. You also pay a monthly insurance fee as part of the loan. If you pay off the loan early, part of the money is refunded.

Rates on FHA loans are comparable to those on conventional loans, but down payments can be as low as 3 percent. FHA loans are aimed at moderate- to lower-income buyers. Nearly 80 percent of FHA borrowers are first-time home buyers. The maximum mortgage varies by region, ranging from $160,176 in low-cost areas to $290,319 in high-cost areas such as California. You can find out more at www.hud.gov.

FHA loans can usually be assumed by a buyer and have lower closing costs than conventional loans. As an added protection for the buyer, the FHA will also inspect the house to make sure that it meets basic structural requirements.

FHA mortgages can be a good selling point for new homes, as a young Mike Sumichrast discovered early in his home-building career.

VA Loans   These are loans made with the backing of the Department of Veteran Affairs. The VA guarantees part of loans made by private lenders. There is a 1 percent funding fee, which can be paid in cash or added to the loan amount. To qualify, you must have been in the military or be the surviving, unmarried spouse of a veteran. You first need to obtain a certificate of eligibility from the VA. A major advantage of VA loans is that you can get them with no down payment up to the mortgage limit of $240,000. You may choose to put some money down in order to hold down the monthly payments, however.

VA loans have many of the benefits of FHA loans. The VA mortgage rate is set by the agency, and the FHA follows suit. Check details at www.homeloans.va.gov.

Mike's Favorite FHA Housing Story

The 354 homes we built at Grandview in Pennsylvania in the 1950s did not sell well at all. So we rented some of them, and turned over the balance, unsold, to the Federal Housing Administration. This was my first exposure to a government project that should never have been built. Lord knows how much money the U.S. government lost.

Our project was not far from the New Jersey border, and while I was working on it, I got one of my first lessons about that part of the world. One night after work, several of us met with other construction workers at a local pub. A superintendent from a nearby project in New Jersey started to tell us his day's progress.

"I was under pressure from my boss in New York to get six final inspections, because we were short of cash and the bank wasn't going to release funds without the FHA inspections.

"I got all six," he said.

"So what is the big deal?" asked one of the construction men.

"I had only three houses finished for final inspections. So I took the old inspector once through the three houses and then back again through the same three houses. He signed all six home inspections."

Fixed Rate or a Call to ARMs?

FIXED-RATE MORTGAGES

These are the old reliable mortgages in which the interest rate and the monthly payments for principal and interest remain level over the life of the loan. When rates are low, it is a good idea to lock in a fixed rate, especially if you expect to be in the house for a long time. Then, as your income grows, your payment becomes a lower percentage of your income.

Fixed-rate loans still account for the bulk of mortgages, despite predictions that they would go the way of the dodo. We aren't surprised. When variable-rate mortgages were becoming the new rage in the late 1970s, we wrote: "To paraphrase Mark Twain, the death of fixed-rate mortgages has been greatly exaggerated."

ADJUSTABLE-RATE MORTGAGES, OR ARMS

These are mortgages that start out with a fixed rate, amortized over 25 or 30 years, but where the rate is eventually adjusted, up or down, as general interest rates change. Initially ARMs were a crapshoot because they were topless; the rates could go up without limit. Under a law that took effect in 1988, however, there must be a cap on rates, although it can be as high as the lender wants.

With ARMS, the mortgage rate stays the same for a certain number of years—2 years, 5 years, 7 years, or even 10 years—but then is adjusted up or down every year based on a predetermined index, such as the cost-of-funds index or the rate on U.S. Treasury bills. For instance, a 5/1 ARM would be adjusted after 5 years.

Generally, such loans have a cap of 5 to 6 percentage points, and annual adjustments are also limited, often to 2 percentage points. The starting rate should be lower than the rate for fixed-rate mortgages. ARMs are good loans to get if you plan to be in a house for only a few years. Otherwise, be sure you could afford the payments if they were ever adjusted up to the max.

Length of Mortgage

The other factor in your mortgage payment is the length of the loan. The longer the mortgage, the lower your monthly payment will be, but also the more interest you will pay over the life of the loan.

Typically mortgages have been for 25 to 30 years. This allows buyers to hold down their monthly payments, pay off the loans with money that has been made less valuable by inflation, and garner tax write-offs. But with lower inflation and tax write-offs, plus the aging population, many buyers prefer to build up equity in their homes more quickly by choosing a 15-year mortgage. With these mortgages, the monthly payment is higher than with a 30-year loan, but the buyer saves thousands of dollars in interest payments. Plus, the buyer owns the house after only 15 years.

The web site www.pickmymortgage.com shows the following comparison of two kinds of mortgages.

30-Year or 15-Year Loan?

- You can choose the standard 30-year fixed rate mortgage or pay off your home loan faster with a 15-year fixed rate mortgage.
- The 30-year mortgage term has lower monthly payments, but your APR will be slightly higher. The 15-year fixed rate mortgage term will have a slightly higher monthly payment, but you will usually pay a lower APR.
- The APR on a 15-year mortgage is about 0.05 to 1.0 percent lower than the standard 30-year mortgage. You will also pay your loan off quicker saving thousands of dollars in total interest charges.
- Review the cost comparison in Table 10-2 for a mortgage loan of $100,000.

Table 10-2 A 15-Year Loan vs. a 30-Year Loan
Review this cost comparison for a mortgage loan of $100,000

	15-Year	**30-Year**
Interest rate (APR):	7.50%	8.00%
Monthly payment:	$927.01	$733.76
Number of payments:	180	360
Total money spent:	$166, 862	$246,149
Total interest paid:	$66,862	$164,149

Source: Crayton Davis, www.pickmymortgage.com.

If you are disciplined, you can effectively shorten the length of your 25- or 30-year mortgage by making extra monthly payments. On many mortgages, making the equivalent of just one extra payment a year can cut the mortgage time in half. This way, you can skip extra payments when you want, say when the holiday bills come due. But you can still reduce the time it takes to pay down your mortgage.

Varieties of Mortgages

These days, lenders have more varieties of mortgage loans than Heinz has varieties of food. Here is just a sample.

Low-down-payment mortgages. You can get a conventional mortgage with little as a 5 or 10 percent down payment by getting private mortgage insurance. The private mortgage insurance company insures the part of the mortgage that is beyond the maximum percentage that the lender would otherwise allow. Thus, if a lender normally would lend no more than 80 percent of a home's price (a 20 percent down payment), you can get a loan for 95 percent of the price (a 5 percent down payment) because the insurance will cover the difference. You pay for this insurance, of course.

Different lenders have different variations on this theme. Wells Fargo, for instance, offers a "No Money Down Plus" mortgage that lets qualified buyers borrow up to 103 percent of the mortgage amount. The program is aimed at people who have good incomes but low savings, or who want to use their savings for other investments.

80-10-10 mortgages. This is another way to avoid private insurance costs. The lender makes one loan for 80 percent of the purchase price, you make a 10 percent down payment, and the remaining 10 percent is financed with a second mortgage or home equity loan. You'll pay a higher rate for the second mortgage, but that mortgage covers only 10 percent of the purchase price.

Convertible mortgages. You can have the best of both mortgage worlds—an adjustable-rate mortgage that can be converted into a fixed-rate mortgage when rates go down. There is a conversion fee, but usually it is cheaper than refinancing. (Be sure to check all fees before you say farewell to ARMs.) This conversion is usually done after a specific number of months.

Two-step mortgage. This is essentially a one-time-only adjustable-rate mortgage. You get a lower rate for the first 5 or 7 years of a 30-year loan, then the rate is adjusted upward one time to a new fixed rate. Again, this is a mortgage to consider if you expect to be in a house for only 5 to 7 years. According to Fannie Mae, which created this type of mortgage, these mortgages are paid off or refinanced after an average of 7 years.

Balloon mortgages. With a balloon mortgage, you have smaller monthly payments (while accumulating more interest charges, of course), but at some predetermined point, perhaps after 5 to 15 years, the balance becomes due—*in full.* At that point you can refinance the loan or, if you have been saving as you planned, pay off the remaining note. Just be sure that if your balloon were to burst at a time of high rates, you could afford your new payments.

Interest-only loans. These loans let you pay only interest and nothing toward the principal of the loan for the first 3 to 10 years. The good news is that this can save you up to 25 percent on your monthly payment, so that you can afford a more expensive home. Plus, all of your mortgage payment is tax-deductible. The bad news is that you aren't paying down your mortgage. Eventually you will have to do so, and your monthly payments will jump up. If housing prices should drop, you could end up owing more than you could get for the house. Again, this is an option for people who don't plan to be in a house for more than 3 to 10 years.

There are scores of other special mortgages. As reported by *Builders* magazine online, these unusual offerings include a "no-cost mortgage," which covers a borrower's costs for a slightly higher interest rate. Another is an Internet lender's "Mortgage on the Move," a portable loan featuring, at an added cost, a one-time option to purchase another home at the same rate with the then-current balance. There are home mortgages with a built-in line of credit for the difference between the value of the home and the purchase loan's principal balance. There is financing combining an 80 percent loan-to-value first mortgage with a 20 percent second mortgage, both at slightly above-market terms, eliminating the need for mortgage insurance.

Fannie Mae has a Community Home Buyer's Program. This is a loan program targeted at home buyers with low or moderate incomes. It requires a down payment of only 5 percent. Buyers can use up to 33 percent of their gross monthly income for housing expenses each month (instead of the standard 28 percent) and 38 percent for their total monthly debt expenses (instead of the standard 36 percent).

Freddie Mac has developed an Islamic Mortgage Initiative to help home-buying Muslims whose religion forbids them to pay interest. Essentially, organizations that make home financing available to Muslim families can sell home-financing contracts to Freddie Mac and recoup their expenses. Freddie Mac forecasts that financing contracts for Muslim families will soon exceed $100 million.

Shopping for a Mortgage

You should shop as hard for your mortgage as you do for your house. Your real estate agent may be able to guide you to a competitive lender, but you should do some checking yourself. A survey by Electronic Realty Associates found that brokers most often recommend the lender with the most efficient service rather than the one with the lowest rate.

You want to find the mortgage with the most favorable interest rate and the lowest charges. How do you do that? What a difference a few years makes! Today you can log onto your favorite computer and access scores of web sites to shop for the best mortgage.

Find out the kinds of loans each lender will make and what size of the down payment is required. Generally, the bigger the down payment or the shorter the loan term, the lower the interest rate.

You need to compare more than the basic mortgage rate, however. Often you will have to pay a certain number of "points." One point equals 1 percent of the mortgage. Thus, if you had to pay one point on a $100,000 mortgage, the cost would be $1000. The lenders call these charges a "loan origination fee" or "discount points." Others simply call them prepaid interest. You pay the money when you go to the closing on your house. The good news is that points are tax-deductible.

Should you try to get a loan with no points? If you don't plan to be in the house for more than 5 years or so, definitely. Paying points should get you a lower interest rate, however, so if you stay in the house for a long time, you will save money with the lower rate and monthly payment.

You will have other costs as well, including application fees. All of this can make it hard to compare different loans. But there are ways to compare apples with apples.

The best way to compare mortgage costs is with the effective percentage rate (APR), which includes not only the interest rate but also costs for points and other fees. The lender must send you a truth-in-lending disclosure statement that includes the APR within 3 days after you apply for a loan. But you can get this information up front. Often, you can get the APR from the lender. You also can find helpful calculator tools on the Internet, such as Fannie Mae's True Cost Calculator at www.homepath.com.

You must compare similar loan products for the same loan amount, as the U.S. Department of Housing and Urban

Development notes. For example, suppose you are comparing two 30-year fixed-rate loans for $100,000. Loan A, with an APR of 8.35 percent, is less costly than Loan B, which has an APR of 8.65 percent over the loan term. However, before you decide on a loan, you should consider the up-front cash that you will be required to pay for each of the two loans as well.

Another effective shopping technique is to compare identical loans with different up-front points and other fees. For example, if you are offered two 30-year fixed-rate loans for $100,000 and at 8 percent, the monthly payments will be the same, but the up-front costs will be different:

Loan A: 2 points ($2000) and lender-required costs of $1800 = $3800 in costs.
Loan B: 2¼ points ($2250) and lender-required costs of $1200 = $3450 in costs.

A comparison of the up-front costs shows that Loan B requires $350 less in up-front cash than Loan A. However, your individual situation (how long you plan to stay in your house) and your tax situation (points can usually be deducted in the tax year in which you purchase a house) may affect your choice of loan.

Applying for a Mortgage

When you go in to apply for a home loan, go prepared. First, be prepared to pay an application fee of a couple of hundred dollars or so. You will also have to pay for an appraisal and a credit report. Other items you will need include a signed sales contract for a house, a copy of a canceled check for your earnest deposit, verification of the source of funds for your down payment, tax forms for the past two years, investment records, records on checking and savings accounts, and records on your monthly debts.

ASK THE LENDER

The lender will then evaluate you for approval of a loan. But you should be evaluating the lender as well. Here is a list of questions from the Department of Housing and Urban Development:

- Is there a late payment charge? How much? How late may the payment be before the charge is imposed?
- If you wish to pay off the loan in advance of maturity (for example, if you move or sell the house), must you pay a prepayment penalty? How much is it? If so, for how long a period will it apply?
- Will the lender permit assumption?
- Will the lender release you from personal liability if your loan is assumed by the buyer when you sell the home?
- If you sell the home and the buyer assumes your loan, will the lender have the right to charge an assumption fee, raise the rate of interest, or require payment of the mortgage in full?

Also, ask if the application fee will be refunded if you aren't approved or if you decide to go someplace else. The Web is full of lenders who are willing to make a deal. So check it out!

Also, check out these options.

- Lock in your rate for a certain period, such as 60 days. You will get this rate if you settle within 60 days. But you must provide requested documentation in a timely fashion when requested.
- "Float" the rate and points, subject to daily changes in market conditions. Choose this option only if the market is going down.
- Ask if you can lock in a rate with one "float down" if the rates drop just before you close on a loan.

Table 10-3 is a mortgage-shopping worksheet from the Federal Reserve Board to help you make your decision.

Table 10-3   Mortgage Shopping Worksheet

	Lender 1		Lender 2	
Name of Lender:				
Name of Contact:				
Date of Contact:				
Mortgage Amount:				
	Mortgage 1	Mortgage 2	Mortgage1	Mortgage 2
Basic Information on the Loans **Type of mortgage: fixed rate, adjustable rate, conventional, FHA, other?** **If adjustable, see below**				
Minimum down payment required				
Loan term (length of loan)				
Contract interest rate				
Annual percentage rate (APR)				
Points (may be called loan discount points)				

(continued)

Table 10-3   (*Continued*)

Monthly private mortgage insurance (PMI) premium				
How long must you keep PMI?				
Estimated monthly escrow for taxes and hazard insurance				
Estimated monthly payment (principal, interest, taxes, insurance, PMI)				
Fees **Different institutions may have different names for some fees and may charge different fees. We have listed some typical fees you may see on loan documents.** **Application fee or loan processing fee**				
Origination fee or underwriting fee				
Lender fee or funding fee				

Table 10-3   (Continued)

Appraisal fee				
Attorney fees				
Document preparation and recording fees				
Broker fees (may be quoted as points, origination fees, or interest-rate add-on)				
Credit report fee				
Other fees				
Other Costs at Closing/Settlement				
Title search/title insurance For lender				
For you				
Estimated prepaid amounts for interest, taxes, hazard insurance, payments to escrow				
State and local taxes, stamp taxes, transfer taxes				
Flood determination				

(continued)

Table 10-3   (*Continued*)

Prepaid private mortgage insurance (PMI)				
Surveys and home inspections				
Total fees and other closing/settlement cost estimates				
	Lender 1		**Lender 2**	
Name of Lender:				
	Mortgage 1	Mortgage 2	Mortgage 1	Mortgage 2
Other Questions and Considerations about the Loan Are any of the fees or costs waivable?				
Prepayment penalties Is there a prepayment penalty?				
If so, how much is it?				
How long does the penalty period last? (for example, 3 years? 5 years?)				
Are extra principal payments allowed?				

Table 10-3 (Continued)

Lock-ins **Is the lock-in agreement in writing?**				
Is there a fee to lock in?				
When does the lock-in occur—at application, approval, or another time?				
How long will the lock-in last?				
If the rate drops before closing, can you lock in at a lower rate?				
If the Loan Is an Adjustable-Rate Mortgage: **What is the initial rate?**				
What is the maximum the rate could be next year?				
What are the rate and payment caps each year and over the life of the loan?				
What is the frequency of rate changes and of any changes to the monthly payment?				

(continued)

Table 10-3 (*Continued*)

What is the index that the lender will use?				
What margin will the lender add to the index?				
Credit Life Insurance **Does the monthly amount quoted to you include a charge for credit life insurance?**				
If so, does the lender require credit life insurance as a condition of the loan?				
How much does the credit life insurance cost?				
How much lower would your monthly payment be without the credit life insurance?				
If the lender does not require credit life insurance, and you still want to buy it, what rates can you get from other insurance providers?				

Sources: Department of Housing and Urban Development, Department of Justice, Department of the Treasury, Federal Deposit Insurance Corporation, Federal Housing Finance Board, Federal Reserve Board, Federal Trade Commission, National Credit Union Administration, Office of Federal Housing, Enterprise Oversight, Office of the Comptroller of the Currency, Office of Thrift Supervision.

Cautionary Tales

Most lenders are honest, and you shouldn't run into problems. But you should keep your guard up for potential abuses.

PREDATORY LENDING

In recent years some lenders have preyed on lower-income buyers who might have a hard time getting a mortgage. These lenders—and unfortunately they have included some major banks—provide such buyers with high-cost loans that they often cannot afford. As a result, the buyers end up losing their homes. Among the tactics used are providing false appraisals for overpriced homes, encouraging borrowers to lie about their income and expenses in order to qualify for a loan, charging excessive fees and mortgage rates, and knowingly lending more money than the borrower can afford to pay.

Congress and many states have moved to pass legislation against predatory lending. But there are things that you can do to protect yourself. Tips from the U.S. Department of Housing and Urban Development include the following:

- Shop for a lender and compare costs. Be suspicious if anyone tries to steer you to just one lender.
- Do *not* let anyone persuade you to make a false statement on your loan application, such as overstating your income or failing to disclose the source of your down payment, the nature and amount of your debts, or even how long you have been employed. Lying on a mortgage application is fraud and may result in criminal penalties.
- Do *not* let anyone convince you to borrow more money than you know you can afford to repay. If you get behind on your payments, you risk losing your house and all of the money you have put into your property.

HOUSING DISCRIMINATION

Another lingering mortgage problem, after all these years, remains discrimination against minorities. Several studies in 2002 and

2003 found that African Americans were often charged higher rates by some mortgage lenders. Minorities also sometimes have a harder time getting loan approvals.

Mike Sumichrast got his first lesson in housing discrimination when he started looking for a place to live in America.

Mike's Not-So-Favorite Housing Bias Story

My first experience with housing discrimination in the United States was in 1955. I called about an apartment in Brooklyn, New York, and the voice on the other end said, "Tell me, are you black or Puerto Rican?"

"Neither," I said.

"OK, then come over."

When Mrs. Sumichrast and I purchased our first house, on Olentangy Boulevard in Columbus, Ohio, in 1957, we heard our neighbors complaining: "What is this neighborhood coming to? We already have a Jew in one house, and now a couple of foreigners are moving in"—meaning us, since I am Czech and Marika was Polish. The fact that the Jew was a world-renowned psychiatrist and that my wife and I, in addition to working, were enrolled in the graduate school at Ohio State University did not make much difference. People simply were afraid of the unknown.

If you think you have been a victim of housing bias, you should contact your state or local housing discrimination agency or the Department of Housing and Urban Development. You can check the www.hud.gov web site to find out what to do.

Hopefully, you won't run into any such problems. In America, home ownership is an equal opportunity dream.

CHAPTER 11

Protecting Yourself at Settlement

The House Is Yours!

Decades ago, Warren Burger, then the chief justice of the United States, declared that the complex system of closing the purchase of a home "cries out for re-examination and simplification."

The chief justice added: "I believe that if American lawyers will put their ingenuity and inventiveness to work on the subject, they will be able to devise simpler methods than we have now."

Calling on lawyers to simplify a complicated legal transaction is like asking Britney Spears to develop a tasteful dress code. The settlement process is still crying out for simplification. In this mystifying ritual, participants often end up signing scores of papers that they don't fully understand.

That can spell trouble, as Mike Sumichrast once discovered.

Figuring Your Closing Costs

The closing, or settlement, of a home purchase is the formal process in which the ownership of the house legally passes from the seller to you, the buyer.

Procedures vary around the country. Generally, on a mutually agreed-upon settlement day, you, the seller, and the closing

---

Mike's Not-So-Favorite Small Print Story

It sounded like a good proposition: Right after the Communists were chased out of Czechoslovakia, build a good-looking U.S. model home in Prague, and people will go wild to buy it—and more. One day we received a call from our head of sales, who informed us that he had sold the model home for a tidy profit. Three days later, the sales manager called back to inform us that the buyer, without the manager's knowledge, had edited the contract in the local language, deleting the words *to be* paid in full and replacing them with *was* paid in full.

The "buyer" then ran down to the local court and transferred the $300,000 home to himself for no money. After spending a lot of money in legal fees for a bunch of lawyers, we just gave up and left, and the fraudulent buyer moved into his new house.

The moral of the story: Know your local laws.

---

attorney whom you hire sit down around a table. (With a newly built home, the seller probably won't be at settlement.)

A lot of papers will be shoved under your nose for you to sign. The only consolation is that it could be worse. Real estate tycoon A. Alfred Taubman's financing of his stake in 17 shopping centers required the signing of 4000 documents.

Many of these papers mean that you are agreeing to disburse payments to the seller, the lender, and others. This brings up an important point: You should be aware that you will have to pay lots of cash at closing. The amount varies depending on the area of the country. You can figure that the cost will total 3 to 5 percent of the purchase price. Thus, for a $150,000 house, you're talking about $4500 to $7500 or more. These costs typically include such items as points, an appraisal cost, a credit report fee, an insurance premium, title insurance, recording and transferring charges, and interest for the period between the closing date and the first mortgage payment you make.

Some officials note that not all of this involves cost to you. A good portion involves depositing money in escrow accounts to make future payments on taxes or insurance. The bottom line, however, is that you must be prepared to pay for these things up front at settlement.

Under the Real Estate Settlement Procedures Act (RESPA), the lender must send you a "good faith" estimate of the closing costs within 3 days after you apply for a mortgage. Unfortunately, too often these estimates aren't as good faith as they should be, and there are continuing efforts to tighten the RESPA requirements. In any case, the law also requires that you receive a list of the actual closing costs at the closing attorney's office at least 1 day before you go to settlement. You should make sure you go over the list of actual costs before going to settlement. The list often has mistakes that may not be in your favor.

But you don't want to wait until then to get a good fix on how much the closing costs will be. You should try to prepare a detailed estimate while you are shopping for a loan, or at least soon after you get a loan commitment.

For help, you can go to www.hud.gov on the Internet, and click on "Calculating the Amount You Need at Settlement." For more details, you can call up "Buying Your Home, Settlement Costs and Useful Information," which runs 24 pages. Or you can use the HUD form reprinted in Table 11-1 to make your estimates.

Saving Money on Closing Costs

Many settlement costs can't be avoided, but there are things you can do to hold down the expense.

- *Shop for closing services.* You have the right to choose the closing attorney. Call several to compare prices.

- *Shop for closing costs in advance.* Don't wait until you get the required disclosures after you have applied for a loan. Shop lenders and compare closing costs.
- *Share the points.* In most places, the seller will pay part of the points the lender charges on your mortgage. In a buyer's market, you may be able to get the seller to pay even more of the closing costs than the points. The seller may agree, for example, to simply pay a certain amount toward closing costs so that he or she can sell the house.
- *Title search.* When you buy a house, the title must be checked to make sure that it isn't defective and that the seller really does own the house. You can reduce the cost and speed the process by having the search done by the same firm that searched the title for the current owner.
- *Title insurance.* Just in case there are any flaws in the title that are not uncovered during the title search, you must buy title insurance for the lender and, if you wish, a separate policy for yourself. If the title insurance on the house you are buying is less than 10 years old or so, you can get a cheaper "reissue rate" from the same title company. If you are buying a newly constructed home, make certain that your title insurance covers claims by contractors. These claims are known as "mechanic's liens" in some parts of the country.
- *Survey.* You can save money by having the survey of the house you are buying done by the same company that did it for the sellers when they bought the house.
- *Homeowner's insurance.* Before you take title to a house, the lender will require that you have a homeowner's insurance policy. If you don't acquire one yourself, a policy will be provided at closing, and you will be charged for it. You can save money by shopping for the best rate and buying a policy yourself.

Going to Closing—Step by Step

Finally the big day is here. You go to the closing on your new house at the office of your closing attorney or title company. Basically, the

closing attorney will finalize your home purchase using the H
1 Settlement Statement that is shown in Table 11-1.

Closing is a complicated procedure, and you should find ou
as much as you can about yours before the day arrives. To help
you protect your rights, the following is a step-by-step explanation of the procedure led by Benny Kass, a veteran real estate
attorney in Washington, D.C., and a longtime columnist for the
Washington Post.

"The first thing is to know that the buyer has the absolute
right to determine where they're going to go to settlement," Mr.
Kass said. "Usually, on new home sales the seller will say that
you have the right to go where you want to go for settlement,
but if you use our settlement attorney, we'll give you x, y, and z
credits. You have to compare the costs of their settlement
lawyer to the alternatives," he said. It could be cheaper to go
elsewhere, even with the credits.

Before going to closing, you should go over your sales contract. You also should have a list of actual closing costs that you
should check for mistakes. In addition, "I strongly recommend
that buyers bring their 'good faith' estimate from the lender to
settlement and compare it" with the actual closing costs, Mr.
Kass said. Don't be afraid to question charges that are more
than the estimate.

Oh, yes, and don't forget to bring a certified check to pay
those closing costs. Don't bring cash. That makes closing attor-
neys nervous, said Roy McKeever, a closing attorney in Maryland:

"I had a gentleman come in late on a Friday, like 6 in the
evening, and he was a big fellow and literally an ominous-look-
ing fellow, and he sat down and did the closing."

At the end of the closing, Mr. McKeever said, his buyer
"reached down under the chair and pulled out a box. It was full
of money. I mean money stacked in there like file cards. It was
like $130,000 in cash."

But at this time of the evening, Mr. McKeever was nearly
alone in the office with his burly client and all the money. "It
scared me to death."

Table 11-1   HUD Settlement Sheet

Buying Your Home
Settlement Costs and Helpful Information
June 1997 Disclaimer
HUD-1 Settlement Statement Costs

A. U.S. DEPARTMENT OF HOUSING AND URBAN DEVELOPMENT SETTLEMENT STATEMENT				
B. TYPE OF LOAN			**6. File Number**	**7. Loan Number**
	1. o FHA	2. o FmHA		
3. o CONV. UNINS.	**4. o VA**	**5. o CONV. INS.**	**8. Mortgage Insurance Case Number**	
C. NOTE: This form is furnished to give you a statement of actual settlement costs. Amounts paid to and by the settlement agent are shown. Items marked "(p.o.c.)" were paid outside the closing; they are shown here for informational purposes and are not included in the totals.				
D. NAME AND ADDRESS OF BORROWER:	**E. NAME AND ADDRESS OF SELLER:**		**F. NAME AND ADDRESS OF LENDER:**	
G. PROPERTY LOCATION:	**H. SETTLEMENT AGENT: NAME, AND ADDRESS**			
	PLACE OF SETTLEMENT:		**I. SETTLEMENT DATE:**	
J. SUMMARY OF BORROWER'S TRANSACTION		**K. SUMMARY OF SELLER'S TRANSACTION**		
100. GROSS AMOUNT DUE FROM BORROWER:		**400. GROSS AMOUNT DUE TO SELLER:**		
101. Contract sales price		**401. Contract sales price**		

Table 11-1 *(Continued)*

102. Personal property		402. Personal property	
103. Settlement charges to borrower (line 1400)		403.	
104.		404.	
105.		405.	
Adjustments for items paid by seller in advance		Adjustments for items paid by seller in advance	
106. City/town taxes to		406. City/town taxes to	
107. County taxes to		407. County taxes to	
108. Assessments to		408. Assessments to	
109.		409.	
112.		412.	
120. GROSS AMOUNT DUE FROM BORROWER		420. GROSS AMOUNT DUE TO SELLER	
200. AMOUNTS PAID BY OR IN BEHALF OF BORROWER:		500. REDUCTIONS IN AMOUNT DUE TO SELLER:	
201. Deposit of earnest money		501. Excess deposit (see instructions)	
202. Principal amount of new loan(s)		502. Settlement charges to seller (line 1400)	
203. Existing loan(s) taken subject to		503. Existing loan(s) taken subject to	
204.		504. Payoff first mortgage loan	
205.		505. Payoff second mortgage loan	

(continued)

Table 11-1 (*Continued*)

206.		506.	
207.		507.	
208.		508.	
209.		509.	
Adjustments for items unpaid by seller		**Adjustments for items unpaid by seller**	
212. Assessments to		512. Assessments to	
213.		513.	
214.		514.	
215.		515.	
216.		516.	
217.		517.	
218.		518.	
219.		519.	
220. TOTAL PAID BY/FOR BORROWER		520. TOTAL REDUCTION AMOUNT DUE SELLER	
300. CASH AT SETTLEMENT FORM/TO BORROWER		600. CASH AT SETTLEMENT TO/FROM SELLER	
301. Gross amount due from borrower (line 120)		601. Gross amount due to seller (line 420)	
302. Less amounts paid by/for borrower (line 220)		602. Less reductions in amount due seller (line 520)	
303. CASH (_ FROM) (_ TO) BORROWER		603. CASH (o TO) (o FROM) SELLER	

Table 11-1 (Continued)

I. SETTLEMENT CHARGES		
700. TOTAL SALES/BROKER'S COMMISSION based on price $ @ % =	PAID FROM BORROWER'S FUNDS AT SETTLEMENT	PAID FROM SELLER'S FUNDS AT SETTLEMENT
Division of Commission (line 700) as follows:		
701. $ to		
702. $ to		
703. Commission paid at Settlement		
704.		
800. ITEMS PAYABLE IN CONNECTION WITH LOAN		
801. Loan Origination Fee %		
802. Loan Discount %		
803. Appraisal Fee to		
804. Credit Report to		
805. Lender's Inspection Fee		
806. Mortgage Insurance Application Fee to		
807. Assumption Fee		
808.		
809.		
810.		
811.		

(continued)

Table 11-1 (*Continued*)

902. Mortgage Insurance Premium for months to		
903. Hazard Insurance Premium for years to		
904.		
905.		
1000. RESERVES DEPOSITED WITH LENDER		
1001. Hazard Insurance months @ $ per month		
1002. Mortgage insurance months @ $ per month		
1003. City property taxes months @ $ per month		
1004. County property taxes months @ $ per month		
1005. Annual assessments months @ $ per month		
1006. months @ $ per month		
1007. months @ $ per month		
1008. Aggregate adjustment months @ $ per month		
1102. Abstract or title search to		
1103. Title examination to		
1104. Title insurance binder to		
1105. Document preparation to		

Table 11-1   (Continued)

1106. Notary fees to		
1107. Attorney's fees to		
(includes above items numbers;)		
1108. Title Insurance to		
(includes above items numbers;)		
1109. Lender's coverage $		
1110. Owner's coverage $		
1111.		
1112.		
1113.		
1200. GOVERNMENT RECORDING AND TRANSFER CHARGES		
1201. Recording fees: Deed $; Mortgage $; Releases $		
1202. City/county tax/stamps: Deed $; Mortgage $		
1205.		
1300. ADDITIONAL SETTLEMENT CHARGES		
1301. Survey to		
1302. Pest Inspection to		
1303.		
1304.		
1305.		
1400. TOTAL SETTLEMENT CHARGES (enter on lines 103, Section J and 502, Section K)		

Source: U.S. Department of Housing and Urban Development.

You also should make one stop on your way to closing on your new house. "The morning of the closing—not the night before, not the day before—you should inspect the house," Mr. Kass advised. If something isn't working, and you catch it, you can say to the seller, "That's not the way it was when I signed the contract; it's your responsibility." Mr. Kass recalled that, "I had one situation where the client called me from the house and said, 'The hot water heater is leaking, and they put chewing gum on it; is that good enough?' I said, 'No, it's not good enough.' We negotiated a $250 to $300 credit."

When you arrive at the closing attorney's office, be prepared to stay for a while. "Make sure that you're not in what I call the diploma mill arrangement, quick here, sign here, because I've got two other people waiting," Mr. Kass advised. "You are entitled to know exactly what is going on. Make sure that you understand each document that you read. If you don't, get an explanation."

Other participants at the closing usually include the seller and any real estate agents involved. You may also have your own attorney at the proceedings. The closing attorney, no matter how neutral he or she may try to be, legally represents the lender.

The closing attorney should go through the HUD-1 form with you. Mr. Kass said he starts by confirming the numbers on page one of the two-page HUD-1 form, which starts with the number 100.

> *Line 101, sales price.* "I ask the buyer and the seller to confirm the sales price," Mr. Kass said. "Then I jump to Line 201."
> *Line 201, deposit.* This is the deposit that the seller put on the house. "I say, 'Who's holding the deposit?'" Mr. Kass said. Usually, it is a third party, not the seller. "You should never give a deposit check to a seller," Mr. Kass said. He recalled the case of a woman in the late 1970s "who took 19 or so contracts for the sale of her Virginia condo, and she took deposit checks. Then she was off to Brazil with all the checks."

After confirming the sales price and the deposit, "then I say to the parties, since this is a good government document, we'll start on page 2 and work our way back," Mr. Kass said.

Line 703, commissions. This is the commission that the seller is paying the real estate agent. "There should be no commission paid by the buyer," Mr. Kass said.

LOAN COSTS

Line 801, loan origination fee. This is also called points. Each point is equal to 1 percent of the sales price. This fee covers the lender's administrative costs for processing the loan. For example, if a lender charges two points on a $120,000 loan, the fee would be $2400. In many jurisdictions, the points are split with the seller. You also may have a loan with no points, in which case there should be no charges on this line.

Line 802, loan discount fee. This is also often called points or discount. It is a one-time charge by the lender or broker to lower the cost at which the lender would otherwise offer the loan to you. Again, you may not be paying any points. If you do pay points, "make sure the points are down there, because points are tax-deductible in the year in which you buy the house," Mr. Kass noted.

Line 803, appraisal fee. The lender hires an appraiser to verify the value of your newly purchased home. You, however, pay for this. Since it's your money, insist on getting a copy of the appraisal. That's very important for a couple of reasons, Mr. Kass said. "It not only shows the value of the house, but if your property happens to be assessed at a higher value than you paid for it, you have the settlement sheet and the appraisal. That should be a slam dunk to lower your property taxes."

Line 804, credit report. You also pay for the lender to run a credit check on you. The lender uses this information to approve your loan.

Line 805, lender's inspection fee. This fee usually applies to a newly built house and is a charge for the representative of the lender to inspect the house.

Line 806, mortgage insurance application fee. If you are making a down payment of less than 20 percent, the lender will get mortgage insurance. You are charged for applying for such coverage for the lender and for the processing of the application.

Line 807, assumption fee. If you are assuming a loan, meaning that you are taking over the duty to pay the seller's existing mortgage loan, the lender will charge you for this transaction.

Lines 808 to 810. "These lines are blank, but lenders conveniently fill them in with what we call 'garbage fees,'" Mr. Kass said. These include fees for document preparation, flood insurance paperwork (even if your house is not in a flood plain), and delivery or messenger charges. These messenger charges can run anywhere from $15 to thousands of dollars, depending "on how far and how often the messengers have to run," complained Mr. McKeever, the Maryland closing attorney.

PREPAID ITEMS

Line 901, interim interest charges. This covers the interest you owe on the mortgage between the time the loan is closed and the time the first payment is due. Be sure to make a note of this payment, Mr. Kass urged. "This is critical because mortgage interest is one of the few things you can deduct for tax purposes. My random sample indicates that 50 percent of lenders, when they send your 1099 tax form at the end of the year, do not include the extra interest because their computer has not been triggered."

Line 902, mortgage insurance premium. If your down payment is less than 20 percent, you will probably have to get private mortgage insurance. At closing, the lender may charge the first-year payment up front in cash.

Line 903, homeowner's insurance premium. The lender will require you to get hazard insurance on the house. You must either show proof that you have a one-year policy or pay for such a policy at the closing. The insurance covers loss due to fire, windstorm, and natural hazards.

Line 904, flood insurance. If a home is in a flood plain, the lender will require flood insurance, which will have to be prepaid.

Line 1001, Homeowner's insurance. Lenders may require you to deposit two months, or $2/12$, of the following year's insurance premium in addition to the one-year premium.

DEPOSITS FOR RESERVES

Line 1002, mortgage insurance (again!). If you have mortgage insurance, the lender will also hold a year's payment, plus a cushion of two months.

Lines 1003 to 1005, property taxes. You get the same treatment on real estate taxes. Usually the first year's taxes are paid in advance by the lender. You are also charged for taxes as part of your monthly payment. After a year, the lender will adjust the overlap, and you can get any overpayment back. If you should sell your house and move before money is paid out, you would get such deposits back.

TITLE CHARGES

Next come charges for making sure that your title is clear of any defects and that the house is owned by the seller. The title search can go back 100 years or more, if the house is that old. You pay for all of this, of course.

Line 1101, settlement fee. This is what you pay the lawyer or title company that is handling your closing for the use of its office.

Lines 1102 to 1104, title fees. You pay the title company for the title search.

Line 1105, document preparation. You have to pay the lender for the cost of preparing all these documents.

Line 1106, notary fee. This fee is charged for the cost of having a person who is licensed as a notary public swear to the fact that the persons named in the documents did, in fact, sign them.

Line 1107, closing attorney's fee. This is what you pay the attorney who is handling the closing. You didn't think she or he did this for nothing, did you?

Some firms wrap up many of these charges into one package rate.

Line 1108, title insurance. This is the cost of title insurance for the mortgage lender. The lender wants to be insured just in case the title search you just paid for missed some hidden defects in the title. This one-time insurance policy protects only the lender. However, you, being the generous soul that you are, pay for the lender's policy. This is one of the most overpriced forms of insurance in captivity because title defects are extremely rare. Years ago the late Senate Banking Committee Chairman William Proxmire of Wisconsin found that less than $1/2$ of 1 percent of all titles proved to have defects.

Line 1110, owner's title insurance. If you want protection from a title defect yourself, you have to buy a separate policy. You aren't covered by the lender's policy. You aren't required to buy an owner's policy, but many buyers do so for the peace of mind that it gives them. Although flaws are hardly ever found in titles, if there is one, it could cost you your house.

Mr. Kass recalled one time when "A client of mine came running to my office; he almost got hit by a car down at the corner.

He had gotten a letter from a water company in Maryland saying, 'It is determined that your house sits over a water and sewer
easement. Please remove your house.'" Mr. Kass first notified the
title insurance company, saying, "You screwed up." "As it turned
out, we didn't know it at the time, but the builder was going belly
up. He and his survey phonied up where the house should have
been. So the survey was false." The result: The title insurance
company paid about $50,000 for a new survey and other legal
papers. It also paid $175,000 to move the pipes and resod the
lawn. "So for the $300 to $500 that my client paid for title insurance, he saved himself a bundle," Mr. Kass said.

If you decide not to purchase a policy, you are entitled to get,
free, a "record policy" showing that the title search was performed.

OTHER CHARGES

Lines 1201 to 1203, transfer charges. These are charges
(1201) by local governments to record the deeds or trust,
by the city and/or county for tax stamps for the deed and
the mortgage (1202); and by the state for state stamps for
the deed and recording (1203). Some of these costs can
often be shared with the seller.

Line 1301, survey. The lender will charge you for having a
survey done to determine the exact location of the house
and the property. "I go over surveys very, very carefully,"
Mr. Kass said. "I've had too many situations where people
didn't realize what their property was. They thought they
saw the land going back 150 yards, and there was a fence
at the end, but their property was only 100 yards. So look at
the survey. And if you don't understand it, ask your settlement attorney to explain it to you. Where is my land?"

Line 1302, pest inspection. There usually must be an inspection to verify that the house is free of termites and other
pests. In some areas of the country, the seller pays the cost.

Lines 1303 to 1305, other. This includes the inspection fee to
cover the cost of evaluation for lead-based paint hazard risks.

FINAL ADJUSTMENTS

Line 1400, total settlement charges. All these charges are added up on the borrower's side of the ledger. This total is then brought back to page 1 of the form.

BACK TO THE TOP

Line 103, settlement charges to borrower. This is the total of the charges from page 2. But you aren't done paying yet.

Lines 106 to 108, adjustments for items paid by seller in advance. The seller probably has already paid property taxes and other assessments for at least part of the year. Naturally, he or she wants this money back from you. The costs are prorated, so you pay these costs for the time the house is yours. The money goes to the seller.

Line 201, deposit or earnest money. This is where you get credited for the money you put down as a deposit to secure the sale. That money is credited to your account and counted toward the purchase price.

Line 202, new loan. This is how much you are borrowing to buy the house. For one brief, shining moment, you have loads of money. The loan is made to you for, say, $150,000, and you hold the check in your hand. But not for long. You sign it over to the seller. That, plus your down payment and earnest money, is the price of the house.

Lines 210 to 212, unpaid items. Just as the seller may have made some tax and other payments in advance, he or she may also have failed to make some payments that are owed. You should know about this ahead of time. It usually involves payments that are due near the time of settlement. These are adjusted so that the seller pays for his or her share based on when he or she owned the house.

THE BOTTOM LINE

Finally, all costs and payments to you are added and subtracted. The result is the cash that you still owe after adding up your mortgage, your down payment, and your earnest money. It usually amounts to several thousand dollars.

At this point, you finally are pretty much done. But don't relax too much. "To me, the settlement is the beginning and the end of the process. If you've got questions, speak now," Mr. Kass said. And be sure to get copies of the settlement papers, either at the settlement or shortly thereafter. "You must have a copy of everything you sign at settlement. It's critical," Mr. Kass said.

You also have to sit there while the closing attorney goes through the seller's side of the HUD-1 form. But the seller's side is usually fairly simple.

FINAL PAPERWORK

Even after the money has changed hands, you're still not done looking at papers. Next, the buyer is given a copy of the federal truth-in-lending statement, in which the lender states the total interest and the annual percentage rate, including charges. As we said, the lender must provide a disclosure of these charges within 3 days after you apply for a loan, and you should try to get the numbers even before you apply.

It is at this point that many buyers really focus for the first time on how much they are paying for their house, including interest over the life of the mortgage. It can be a shock. For example, a $140,000 mortgage at a 6 percent annual interest rate over 30 years actually costs you more than $420,000. The critical documents in the transaction are the promise to pay the money back to the lender, the security for the promise, and the deed to the house.

The deed is recorded first in the land record, which evidences the transfer of the title from seller to buyer. Then the deed of trust is recorded, indicating that the title was transferred to a new owner.

If you run into any serious problems after the closing or if you have any complaints about the charges you paid, the first place to raise them is with the closing attorney or the lender. If you can't get satisfaction, complain to the appropriate state or local agency. If your complaint charges violation of the Real Estate Settlement Procedure Act of 1974, you should send copies to:

U.S. Department of Housing and Urban Development
Director: Office of Insured Single Family Housing
Attention: RESPA
451 Seventh Street, S.E.
Washington, D.C. 20410

If you still can't get your problem resolved and you think you have suffered monetary damages, you can sue. Any suit charging violation of RESPA must be brought within 1 year from the date on which the alleged violation occurred. RESPA basically covers illegal kickbacks or fees or requiring a buyer to use a particular title insurer. You can also sue under other federal or state laws.

In most cases, though, none of this is necessary. Closing generally goes smoothly, and the ending is usually a happy one.

The House Is Yours

After you have signed all of the papers and paid all of the costs, the big moment arrives for just about all buyers: You are handed the keys. Congratulations. You have just purchased a home.

Index

A

Adjustable-rate mortgages (ARMs), 65, 199
Affordability, 19–45
  and closing costs, 35
  in different areas of country, 39, 41–45
  and down payment size, 23–26
  and homeowner's insurance, 33–34
  and interest rates, 26–29
  and moving costs, 35
  and personal debt, 29–30
  and private mortgage insurance, 34–35
  and property taxes, 30–33
  ratio for, 8, 9
  as reason for continuing sales growth,
    11–12
  of renting vs. buying, 38–41
  28 percent rule for, 20–23
  worksheet for, 35–38
"Affordable" new homes, 51
Ahluwalia, Gopal, 91
American Dream Down Payment Initiative,
  66
American Society of Home Inspectors web
  site, 79–80
AmeriDream Charity Inc., 65
Appliances:
  checklist for, 98
  cost of operating, 147
  life expectancy of, 102
  in older homes, 101
Application fees, mortgage, 204
Appreciation, 112

Asphalt roofs, 127–128
Assessments:
  for community associations, 146–147
  for condos, 171–172
Attic, checklist for, 98
Auctions, house, 61
Auto insurance, 34

B

Baby boom generation, 12
Backup contracts, 182
Balloon mortgages, 202
Bank of America web site, 82
Bankrate.com, 81
Basements:
  checklist for, 98
  evaluation of, 142, 148, 152–153
  life expectancy of, 107
Bathrooms:
  evaluation of, 136–137
  life expectancy of, 102
  in old houses, 50
  size of, 91
Bedrooms, evaluation of, 137
Berson, David, 14
Bestplaces.net, 80
Better Business Bureau web site, 80
Bid4assets web site, 61
Bidding strategy, 183–185
Borrowing (for down payments), 25
Brokaw, Tom, 10–11
Bruss, Robert J., 85

Builders:
BBB information on, 80
discount mortgages offered by, 67–68
discounts prices from, 51–52
reputation of, 16
top 15, 92
Burger, Warren, 215
Bush, George W., 66
BusinessWeek web site, 83
Buyer's agents, 119
Buyer's market, 180
Buyer's rights, 189–190
Bylaws, condo, 174

C
Cabinetry, life expectancy of, 102
Calcara, Frank, 180
Carpentry, quality of, 95
Carter, Jimmy, 69
CC&Rs (Covenants, Conditions &
Restrictions, 170
Cedar shingle roofs, 128–129
Ceilings:
evaluation of, 147, 149–150
in older homes, 101
Celebrity homes, 81
Census Bureau web site, 76–77
Centex, 91
Certificate of occupancy, 98
Chandeliers, 55
Checklists:
for construction quality, 147–149
for evaluating lenders, 206–212
for exterior evaluation of home, 129–132
for interior evaluation of home, 154–158
for presettlement walk-through, 95–98
Cities:
most/least drivable, 116
safest/most dangerous, 115
web sites for researching, 80
Closet systems, life expectancy of, 103
Closing (*see* Settlement)
Closing costs, 35
figuring, 215–217
saving money on, 217–218
CNN-*Money* web site, 84–85
Co-borrowers (for down payments), 25
Commercial banks, mortgages from, 195
Community Association Institute, 170
Community Home Buyer's Program, 203
Commuting time, 99, 116
Comparable houses, 80, 183
Concessions, asking for, 184
Condominiums and town houses,
159–177
information needed before buying,
170–175
as investments, 161–166

Condominiums and town houses (*Cont.*)
lifestyle and rules with, 166–168
prices of, 164
questions to ask about, 175–177
shopping for, 168–169
size of homes vs., 161
as starter homes, 59
types of, 159–160
Conforming loans, 196
Construction quality, 147–149, 168–169
Consumer preferences, 90, 142–146
Conventional mortgages, 196
Convertible mortgages, 202
Cooperatives (co-ops), 160 (*See also*
Condominiums and town houses)
Cost of living, web sites for researching, 80
Costs:
closing, 215–218
for condo associations, 169
of existing home repairs, 99
hidden, for new homes, 94
of land, 5, 6
of living in a house, 146–147
of mortgages, comparing, 204–205
of new vs. existing home operation, 89
Countertops, life expectancy of, 103
Countrywide Financial web site, 82
Covenants, Conditions & Restrictions
(CC&Rs), 170
Credit criteria (for FHA loans), 64
Crime rates, researching, 74, 80, 114–116

D
D. R. Horton, 91, 92
Debt, personal (*see* Personal debt)
Declaration (condominiums), 173
Deed, 233
Del Webb, 91
Demographics, housing gains and, 12–13
Department of Education web site, 77
Department of Housing and Urban
Development (HUD):
communal living study by, 166–168
foreclosures from, 60–61
lender-shopping tips from, 213
subsidy information from, 69
teachers and police officers home-buying
assistance from, 67
web site of, 60, 74
Department of Veterans Affairs, 76 (*See also*
Veterans Administration mortgages)
Design trends, 91
Dining rooms, evaluation of, 142
Disclosures, 189–190
Discrimination in housing, 213–214
Distance from town, price of home and,
56
Domania.com, 80–81

Doors, 55, 97
Down payments:
  affordability of home and size of, 23–26
  allowable sources for, 25–26
  assistance with, 65–66
  for FHA loans, 64
  for foreclosures, 61
  large, 62–63
  monthly payments and size of, 62–63
  no-down-payment VA loans, 63–64
  with private mortgage insurance, 64
  small, 63
Downspouts, checklist for, 126–127
Drainage:
  checklist for, 124
  for new homes, 94
Driveways, heated, 91
Duplexes, 59–60

E
"Echo-boom" generation, 12
80-10-10 loans, 65, 201–202
Electrical systems:
  evaluation of, 148
  life expectancy of, 103
Energy efficiency, 143
Environmental costs, 6
Equity in home (see Home equity)
Existing homes, 87–88, 98–109
  advantages of, 98–99
  cost of new homes vs., 49–50
  disadvantages of, 99–101
  fixer-uppers, 50–51
  inflation and prices of, 2–4
  and life expectancy of parts of home,
    102–109
  median prices for, 8, 9
  new homes vs., 87–88
  price-income ratio for, 8, 9
  sizes of, 87, 88
Exterior evaluation of home, 111–132
  checklist for, 97, 129–132
  commuting time, 116
  convenience to shopping, 117
  crime rate, 113–116
  drainage, 124
  finishes (siding), 124–126
  future area changes, 117–118
  garages, 126
  gutters/downspouts, 126–127
  neighborhood, 111–112
  with real estate agent, 119–120
  roof, 127–129
  school system, 112–114
  style of house, 120–121
  without professional help, 118–119
Extremes, avoiding, 55

F
Family rooms, evaluation of, 137, 141
Fannie Mae:
  Community Home Buyer's Program,
    203
  down payment assistance from, 66
  energy efficiency tips from, 143
  mortgage calculator from, 20
  mortgages bought by, 195–196
  web site of, 20, 73
Federal Bureau of Investigation web site,
  77
Federal government web sites, 74–77
Federal Housing Administration (FHA)
  loans, 197
  advantage of, 64
  down payment for, 64
  Home-Stretch loans with, 66
  as percent of monthly income, 20
Federal Reserve Board web site, 76
Federal Trade Commission (FTC) web site,
  76
Fencing, 93, 95
FHA loans (see Federal Housing
  Administration loans)
Fiberglass shingle roofs, 127–128
Finishes:
  checklist for, 97
  life expectancy of, 103
First-time buyers, subsidies for, 69
5-and-1 ARM, 65
Fixed-rate mortgages, 198–199
Fixer-uppers, 50–51
Fixtures, checklist for, 98
Floor plan, importance of, 15–16
Flooring:
  checklist for, 97
  evaluation of, 151
  heated, 91
  life expectancy of, 104
Footings, life expectancy of, 104
For sale by owner (FSBO), 57, 81
Foreclosed homes, 60–61
Foundations, life expectancy of, 104
Freddie Mac:
  foreclosures from, 61
  inspection checklist from, 149–150
  Islamic Mortgage Initiative, 203
  mortgages bought by, 195–196
  web site of, 61, 72–73
Free Republic, 14
Front doors, 55
FSBO (see For sale by owner)
FTC web site, 76

G
Garages, 122–123, 126

Garden condominium apartments, 160
General Services Administration (GSA) web
    site, 76
Gifts (for down payments), 25
Gimmicks, avoiding, 55
Ginnie Mae:
    mortgages bought by, 195–196
    web site of, 74–75
GMAC Mortgage Corp., 66
GoneHome.com, 81
Government web sites, 74–77
Grading, 96–97, 123
GSA web site, 76
Gutters, checklist for, 97, 126–127

H
Habitat for Humanity International, 69
HART (see Housing Action Resource Trust)
Heated flooring/driveways, 91
Heating, ventilation, and air conditioning
    (HVAC), 104–105
High-rise condominium apartments, 159
HOAs (see Homeowners' associations)
Home equity, 48
    building, 62
    as source of down payment, 48
    sweat equity, 68–69
Home improvements:
    return on investment for, 50
    web sites for researching, 74
Home inspections:
    need for, 16
    for older homes, 100–101
    web sites for inspectors, 79–80
Home ownership, 13–14
    renting vs., 39–41
    web site data on, 74
Home warranties, 99
Home-buying mistakes, 15–16
Homeowners' associations (HOAs), 174–175
Homeowner's insurance, 33–34, 218
Homesteps.com, 73
Homestore Inc. web site, 77
Homestore.com, 74
Home-Stretch loans, 66
Homework for home buying, 15, 56,
    180–181
Hot water heaters, evaluation of,
    153–154
Housing Action Resource Trust (HART),
    65–66
Housing Affordability Index, 26–27
Housing discrimination, 213–214
Housing markets:
    slump-market buying, 58
    types of, 179–180
    web sites for researching, 74

HUD (see Department of Housing and
    Urban Development)
HVAC (see Heating, ventilation, and air
    conditioning)

I
IbidCo web site, 61
Illegal immigrants, 14
Immigration, demand for housing and,
    14–15
Improvements:
    return on investment for, 50
    web sites for researching, 74
Income:
    changes in, over time, 7
    and region of country, 42–44
    and 28 percent rule, 20–23
Individual retirement accounts (IRAs), 25,
    67
Inflation, housing as hedge against, 2–4
Inheritance funds (for down payments),
    25
Inspections (see Home inspections)
Insulation:
    evaluation of, 151–152
    life expectancy of, 105
    in older homes, 101
Insurance:
    homeowner's, 33–34, 218
    private mortgage, 34–35, 64–65
    saving on, 34
    title, 218
Interest rates:
    and affordability of home, 26–29
    changes in, 194–195
    and length of mortgage, 62
    for second mortgages, 67
    on 30- vs. 15-year loans, 200
    web sites for researching, 81
    (See also Mortgages)
Interest-only mortgages, 62, 202
Interior evaluation of home, 133–158
    appliances, 147
    basements, 142, 152–153
    bathrooms, 136–137
    bedrooms, 137
    ceilings, 149–150
    and characteristics of new single-family
        homes, 138–140
    checklist for, 154–158
    consumer preference items,
        143–146
    cost of living in house, 146–147
    dining rooms, 142
    energy efficiency, 143
    family rooms, 137, 141
    floors, 151

Interior evaluation of home (*Cont.*)
  hot water heaters, 153–154
  insulation, 151–152
  kitchens, 133–136
  living rooms, 141–142
  quality of construction, 147–149
  walls, 149–150
  windows, 150–151
Internet shopping, 71–85
  databases of information, 80–81
  Fannie Mae web site, 73
  for foreclosures, 60–61
  Freddie Mac web site, 72–73
  government web sites, 74–77
  and home selling prices, 56
  lender web sites, 81–83
  National Association of Realtors web site,
    73–74
  online auctions, 61
  periodicals' web sties, 83–85
  for specific types of homes, 61
  trade group web sites, 77–80
Investments, homes as, 1–17
  biggest mistakes in home buying, 15–16
  compared to other investments, 16–17
  continuing sales pattern, 8–10
  predicted price crash, 10–11
  reasons for continuing sales growth, 11–15
  reasons for increasing prices, 4–7
  recent rise in prices, 1–4
IRAs (*see* Individual retirement accounts)
Islamic Mortgage Initiative, 203

J
Jumbo loans, 196

K
Kass, Benny, 219, 226–228, 230–231, 233
Kaufman, Al, 193
KB Home, 91, 92
Kennedy, Ethel and Robert F., 19
Kick-out clause, 182
Kiplinger's magazine web site, 84
Kitchens:
  evaluation of, 133–136
  gimmicks for improving looks of, 55
  in old houses, 50
  size of, 91

L
Landscaping, 123
  of existing homes, 99
  life expectancy of, 106
  of new homes, 93
Laundry rooms, 91
Lawyers, buyers', 189
Leasing to buy, 59

Lenders, 194–196
  BBB information on, 80
  competing, 82–83
  evaluating, 206–212
  foreclosures from, 61
  major U.S., 195
  Mortgage Bankers Association web site,
    77–79
  preapproval from, 46
  and predatory lending, 213
  web sites of, 81–83
Lending Tree, 82–83
Lennar Corp, 91, 92
Lereah, David, 166
Levitt homes, 49
Life expectancy of parts of house,
  102–109
Lifestyle amenities, 90, 142–146
Lighting, outside, 55
Living rooms:
  and design trends, 91
  evaluation of, 141–142
Loans (for down payments), 25 (*See also*
  Mortgages)
Local government web sites, 77
Local newspapers, online, 85
Location:
  for condos, 168
  and convenience to shopping, 117
  importance of, 15
  and price appreciation, 112
  (*See also* Neighborhoods)
Lone Ranger house shopping approach,
  118–119
Lot size, 91–93, 99, 123
Low offers, 58
Low-down-payment mortgages, 201
Lower-income buyers, subsidies for, 69
Low-rise condominium apartments, 160

M
Madonna, 19, 81
Magazine web sites, 83–85
Manufactured homes, 60, 74
Manufactured Housing Institute web site,
  79
Markets (*see* Housing markets)
Masonry, life expectancy of, 106
Master deed, 173–174
MBA web site (*see* Mortgage Bankers
  Association web site)
McKeever, Roy, 219
Mills, Jim, 182
Millwork, life expectancy of, 106
Mistakes in home buying, 15
MLS (*see* Multiple Listing Service)
Mobile homes, 60

Money magazine web site, 84–85
Mortgage Bankers Association (MBA) web
   site, 77–79
Mortgage calculations:
  on Fannie Mae web site, 73
  on Ginnie Mae web site, 74, 76
  by hand, 28–29
  online, 20
Mortgage on the Move, 203
Mortgage101.com, 83
Mortgages, 193–214
  adjustable-rate, 199
  applying for, 205–212
  assuming, 57–58
  from builders, 67–68
  conventional, 196
  80-10-10 loans, 65
  fixed-rate, 198–199
  and housing discrimination,
    213–214
  interest rates on, 193–195
  interest-only, 62
  length of, 61–62, 199–201
  nonconventional, 196–198
  for owner/occupant rentors, 60
  piggy-backed, 65
  points for, 204
  preapproval for, 48
  and predatory lending, 213
  second, 67
  shopping for, 203–205, 207–212
  and size of down payment, 23–26
  sources of, 194–196
  for teachers and police officers, 67
  and 28 percent rule, 20–23
  varieties of, 201–203
  web sites for researching, 81
Moving costs, 35
MSN House and Home data site, 71
Multiple Listing Service (MLS),
    73, 119

N

National Association of Home Builders
    (NAHB):
  presettlement walk-through checklist
    from, 95–98
  web site of, 77
National Association of Home Inspectors
    web site, 79
National Association of Realtors:
  Housing Affordability Index, 26–27
  web site of, 73–74
National Association of State Housing
    Agencies, 69
Negotiating deals, 179–191
  buyer's rights, 189–190

Negotiating deals (*Cont.*)
  making offers, 182–185
  and need for lawyers, 189
  skills for, 180–181
  and types of housing markets, 179–180
  writing contracts, 184, 186–189
  (*See also* Strategies for home buying)
Nehemiah Corporation, 65
Neighborhoods:
  of existing homes, 99
  future of, 54, 99, 117–118
  and price appreciation, 112
  turnaround, 52–54
  web sites for researching, 74, 80, 81
NeighborhoodScout.com, 81
New homes, 87–98
  advantages of, 88–92
  "affordable," 51
  characteristics of from 1987–2002,
    138–140
  consumer preferences in, 144–145
  cost of existing homes vs., 49–50
  disadvantages of, 92–96
  finished but unsold, 51–52
  inflation and prices of, 2–4
  median prices for, 8, 9
  most frequent complaints about, 93
  presettlement walk-through checklist,
    96–98
  price-income ratio for, 8, 9
  and reputation of builder, 16
  sizes of, 87–88
  web sites for researching, 74
Newspaper web sites, 83–85
No-down-payment VA loans, 63–64
Nonconventional mortgages, 196–198
Normal housing market, 180
NVR, 91, 92

O

Offers:
  bidding strategies, 183–185
  low, 58
  making, 182–185
  of more than asking price, 59
  options for, 181–182
Off-season buying, 56–57
Older homes:
  and life expectancy of parts of house,
    102–109
  problems with, 100
  as starter homes, 49–50
Online auctions, 61
Online loans, 195
Outside evaluation (*see* Exterior evaluation
    of home)
Owner/occupants, mortgages for, 60

Owners, buying directly from, 57
Ownership of homes (*see* Home ownership)

P
Paints, life expectancy of, 106
Parents, down payment assistance from,
    66–67
Personal debt:
    and amount of mortgage, 29–30
    reducing, 48
Pickmymortgage.com, 200
Pinhole leaks, 149
PITI (*see* Principal, interest, taxes, insurance)
Plumbing:
    evaluation of, 147, 149
    life expectancy of, 107
    in older homes, 100
PMI (*see* Private mortgage insurance)
Points, 204
Police officers, HUD home prices for, 67
Population, sale of homes and, 12, 14
Potential of homes, 54
Preapproval, mortgage, 48
Predatory lending, 213
Presettlement walk-through (*see* Walk-
    through inspection)
Price-income ratio, 8, 9
Prices of homes:
    appreciation of, 112
    condominiums and town houses, 163–165
    and continuing home sales, 8
    in different areas of country, 39, 41–45
    and distance from town, 56
    in first sections of subdivisions, 55
    median, 8, 9
    new vs. existing homes, 49–50, 92
    predicted crash in, 10–11
    ratio of income to, 8, 9
    reasons for increases in, 4–7
    recent rise in, 1–4
    and return on investment, 17
    and unit pricing, 57
    web sites for researching, 74, 80–81
Principal, interest, taxes, insurance (PITI),
    20
    homeowner's insurance, 33–34
    interest rates, 26–29
    principal, 23–26
    property taxes, 30–33
Private mortgage insurance (PMI), 34–35,
    64–65
Professional inspections (*see* Home inspec-
    tions)
Property taxes, 30–33
    cost of, 146
    for existing homes, 99

Pulte Homes, 91, 92
Punch list, 95

R
Radon, 148–149
Rbuy web site, 61
Real estate agents/agencies:
    BBB information on, 80
    and negotiation skills, 182–183
    working with, 119–120
Real Estate Settlement Procedures Act
    (RESPA) of 1974, 217, 234
Realtors, 183
RealtyBid International web site, 61
Region of country, price variation and, 41–45
Regulatory costs, 6
Remodeling Contractor magazine, 50
Renting:
    buying vs., 39–41
    of duplex units, 59–60
    rent vs. own calculator, 78
    saving money while, 48
Resale right (condos), 174
Research for home buying, 15, 56, 180–181
RESPA (*see* Real Estate Settlement
    Procedures Act of 1974)
Retaining walls, 101
Retirement funds (for down payments), 25
Return on investment, 17, 50
Rights of buyers, 189–190
Roofs:
    checklist for, 97, 127–129
    life expectancy of, 107
    of older homes, 100
Rough structures, life expectancy of, 107
Ryan Homes, 92
Ryland Group, 91, 92

S
Sales contract:
    backup, 182
    for condominiums, 173
    writing, 184, 186–189
Sales of homes:
    condominiums and town houses, 162, 163
    continuing rise in, 8–10
    reasons for positive forecast for, 11–15
    taxes on, 69
Saving for home buying, 47–48
Savings and loans, mortgages from, 195
Scams, housing, 76
School systems:
    and location of home, 94
    researching, 112–114
    web sites for researching, 74, 80, 81
Second mortgages, 67
Security appliances, life expectancy of, 105

Seller's market, 180
Senior housing, web sites for researching, 74
Settlement, 215–234
    closing costs, 215–218
    HUD settlement sheet, 220–233
    procedure for, 218–219, 226–234
    walk-through inspection prior to, 95
Shopping, convenience to, 117
Shrewdness, attempt at, 15
Shutters, life expectancy of, 107
Siding:
    checklist for, 124–126
    life expectancy of, 108
    preferences in, 123
Size of homes:
    condominiums vs. single-family, 161
    new vs. existing homes, 87–88
Slate roofs, 128
Slumps, buying during, 58
Small homes (as starters), 49
Smart Money web site, 84
Smoke detectors, 148
Sperling, Bert, 80
Stains, life expectancy of, 106
State government web sites, 77
Strategies for home buying, 47–70
    adjustable-rate mortgages, 65
    "affordable" new homes, 51
    assuming mortgages, 57–58
    auctioned homes, 61
    avoiding gimmicks/extremes, 55
    bidding, 183–185
    condos, 59
    current home equity, 48–49
    direct-from-owner buying, 57
    discounts from builders, 67–68
    doing your homework, 56
    duplex homes, renting part of, 59–60
    FHA loans, 64
    fixer-uppers, 50–51
    foreclosed homes, 60–61
    future of home/neighborhood, 54
    getting in early, 55
    help with down payment, 65–67
    houses farther out, 56
    houses that need work, 50
    interest-only mortgages, 62
    leasing to buy, 59
    length of mortgage, 61–62
    low offers, 58
    mobile homes, 60
    mortgage preapproval, 48
    no-down-payment VA loan, 63–64
    offers over asking price, 59
    off-season buying, 56–57
    older houses, 49–50

Strategies for home buying, (*Cont.*)
    piggybacked loans, 65
    private mortgage insurance, 64–65
    reducing personal debt, 48
    saving money, 47–48
    second mortgages, 67
    size of down payment, 62–63
    slump-market buying, 58
    starting small, 49
    subsidies, 69
    sweat equity, 68–69
    for teachers and police officers, 67
    trading down, 69–70
    trading up, 49
    turnaround neighborhoods, 52–54
    unit pricing buying, 57
    unsold but finished new houses, 51–52
    using IRA money, 67
Streets, noise level of, 121, 122
Structural checkpoints, 147–149
Styles of homes, 120–121
Subdivisions, first section prices in, 55
Subsidies, housing, 69
Surfaces, checklist for, 98
Sweat equity, 68–69
Swimming pools, return on investment in,
    50

T
Taubman, A. Alfred, 216
Taxes:
    deductions for home owners, 13, 30, 32
    on home profits, 69
    property, 30–33
Teachers, HUD home prices for, 67
Termites:
    evaluation for, 148
    in older homes, 100
3-and-1 ARM, 65
Title insurance, 218
Toll Brothers, 91, 92
Town houses (*see* Condominiums and town
    houses)
Trade group web sites, 77–80
Trading down, 69–70
Trading up, 49
Trust funds (for down payments), 25
Truth-in-lending statement, 233
Turnaround neighborhoods, 52–54
28 percent rule, 20–23
Two-step mortgages, 202

U
Unit pricing, 57
Urban, Jeff, 88–89
Utility bills, 146

V

Veterans Administration (VA) mortgages, 197
   no-down-payment loans, 63–64
   as percent of monthly income, 20
   web site for, 76
Views, protected, 94

W

Walk-through inspection:
   checklist for, 96–98
   for new homes, 95
Wall coverings, 55
Wall Street Journal web site, 83–84
Walls:
   evaluation of, 147, 149–150
   life expectancy of, 108
   in older homes, 101
Washington Mutual web site, 82
Water problems, 100
Waterproofing, life expectancy of, 103

Weekley, David, 15
Wells Fargo Bank, 82, 196
Wetzel, Steve, 47
White House web site, 77
Window treatments, life expectancy of, 108
Windows:
   checklist for, 97
   evaluation of, 147, 150–151
   life expectancy of, 108
   in older homes, 101
Wiring, 91
   evaluation of, 148
   life expectancy of, 103
   in older homes, 101
Wood shake roofs, 128–129
Workmanship, quality of, 95
Worksheet, affordability, 36–38

Y

Yards, 123

About the Authors

MICHAEL SUMICHRAST

Michael Sumichrast is the author of several books, including *Planning Your Retirement Housing* (Scott, Foresman & Company for the American Association of Retired Persons), *Where Will You Live Tomorrow?* (Dow Jones-Irwin), and *The Complete Book of Home Buying* (Dow-Jones Books, hardback; Bantam Books paperback). Other publications include *Housing Markets* (Dow Jones-Irwin), *Opportunities in Building Construction Trades* (VGM Career Horizons), and numerous other books, papers, and articles. The fourth edition of *Opportunities in Financial Careers* (McGraw-Hill Trade) was published in March 2004. Michael Sumichrast has written a weekly column for the *Washington Post* and housing-oriented articles for the *Washington Star*. Dr. Sumichrast's autobiography, *Rebirth of Freedom, From Nazis and Communists to a New Life in America*, was first published in Slovak in Bratislava, Slovakia, in 1996, and then in the United States in 1999 by Hellgate Press, with a foreword by General Alexander M. Haig, Jr. Dr. Sumichrast has participated in building over 3000 homes in Australia and the United States. He was the chief economist of the National Association of Home Builders from 1962 to 1987. He holds an M.B.A. and a Ph.D. from Ohio State University and has worked in various capacities for home builders in the United States and abroad.

RONALD G. SHAFER

Ronald G. Shafer was a reporter and features editor at the *Wall Street Journal* for 38 years. He joined the *Journal* in Chicago in 1963, moved to the Detroit bureau in 1964, and in 1968 transferred to the Washington bureau, where he covered housing and consumer affairs. He became a features editor in 1977, and for two decades he also wrote the page 1 column "Washington Wire." In 1990 he was nominated for the Pulitzer Prize for a page 1 story on the drug-related death of his teenage son, Ryan. Mr. Shafer is the coauthor of several books, including *How to Get Your Car Repaired Without Getting Gypped*, with Margaret Carlson (Simon & Schuster), *The Complete Book of Home Buying*, with Michael Sumichrast (Dow Jones Books), and *Planning Your Retirement Housing*, with Michael Sumichrast (Scott, Foresman & Co.). He also edited a paperback book, *Minor Memos* (Andrews & McMeel), a collection of humorous one-liners from his "Washington Wire" column. He has written articles for publications including *Sports Illustrated*, *Reader's Digest*, and *Washingtonian* magazine. Mr. Shafer is a 1962 graduate of Ohio State University, where he was editor-in-chief of the campus newspaper. He currently is a freelance writer and speaker on political humor. He lives in Leesburg, Virginia, with his wife, Mary Rogers.

MARTIN A. SUMICHRAST

Martin A. Sumichrast is a born entrepreneur and business builder. In 1980, as a junior in college, he began working with his father, Dr. Michael Sumichrast, in a real estate development business. In the late 1990s, Martin Sumichrast's career turned to investment banking and the securities business. In 1993, at the age of 26, he started his first publicly traded company, Global Capital Partners, which he grew into a multinational, full-service investment banking firm. In early 2000, the company employed over 300 people in 9 countries and managed more than $1 billion for over 40,000 customers. Mr. Sumichrast has also served on the boards of various private and public companies. He now manages a private venture capital and business advisory firm, Lomond International, Inc., based in Charlotte, North Carolina. He is also coauthor of *Opportunities in Financial Careers*.